SEMINAR STUDIES IN HISTORY

Editor: Patrick Richardson

FREE TRADE AND PROTECTION

SEMINAR STUDIES IN HISTORY

Editor: Patrick Richardson

A full list of titles in this
series will be found on the
back cover of this book

SEMINAR STUDIES IN HISTORY

FREE TRADE AND PROTECTION

Barry Turner

LONGMAN

LONGMAN GROUP LIMITED
London

ASSOCIATED COMPANIES, BRANCHES AND
REPRESENTATIVES THROUGHOUT THE WORLD

© Longman Group Ltd 1971

First published 1971

ISBN 0 582 31424 0

PRINTED IN GREAT BRITAIN BY
WESTERN PRINTING SERVICES LTD, BRISTOL

Contents

Introduction to the Series

The seminar method of teaching is being used increasingly in VI forms and at universities. It is a way of learning in smaller groups through discussion, designed both to get away from and to supplement the basic lecture techniques. To be successful, the members of a seminar must be informed, or else—in the unkind phrase of a cynic—it can be a 'pooling of ignorance'. The chapter in the textbook of English or European history by its nature cannot provide material in this depth, but at the same time the full academic work may be too long and perhaps too advanced for students at this level.

For this reason we have invited practising teachers in universities, schools and colleges of further education to contribute short studies on specialised aspects of British and European history with these special needs and pupils of this age in mind. For this series the authors have been asked to provide, in addition to their basic analysis, a full selection of documentary material of all kinds and an up-to-date and comprehensive bibliography. Both these sections are referred to in the text, but it is hoped that they will prove to be valuable teaching and learning aids in themselves.

Note on the System of References:

A bold number in round brackets (**5**) in the text refers the reader to the corresponding entry in the Bibliography section at the end of the book.

A bold number in square brackets, preceded by 'doc.' [**docs 6, 8**] refers the reader to the corresponding items in the section of Documents, which follows the main text.

PATRICK RICHARDSON
General Editor

Acknowledgements

We are grateful to the following for permission to reproduce copyright material:

The British Museum for letter from Balfour to Duke of Devonshire, 1903, *Balfour Papers*; His Grace the Duke of Devonshire for letter from Duke of Devonshire to Balfour, *Balfour Papers*; Her Majesties Stationery Office for an extract from Proposed Draft of Dispatch to Governors of Self Governing Colonies, *Balfour Papers*; Hutchinson Publishing Group Ltd. for extracts from *My Political Life* by L. S. Amery and *Arthur James Balfour* by Blanch Dugdale.

Part One

THE GOSPEL OF
FREE TRADE

1 The Birth of the Idea

What is highly valuable but of hardly any practical use? This sounds like a Christmas cracker riddle and the answer—gold—immediately suggests that the questioner is playing with words. Gold must be useful, people argue, otherwise it would not cost so much. Yet apart from wedding rings and tooth fillings there is not much to be said for the yellow metal except that from time immemorial traders have accepted it as an international currency. The monetary system of every major country was originally founded on gold and even today world traders like the United States, Britain and France keep vast stocks just to maintain foreign confidence in their paper dollars, pounds and francs. It is one factor in the process of maintaining smooth trade relations with foreign countries on whose custom these States depend for their relatively high standard of living.

But in the Middle Ages the accumulation of precious metals was a matter of the highest national priority taking precedence over such apparently mundane business as providing adequate food for the population. The prosperity of a country was judged not so much on the standard of living of its inhabitants, but more on the quantity of gold and silver stored in the vaults of the exchequer. These metals represented prestige and the ability to survive a major war, when they could be used to buy military equipment and the services of professional soldiers. As a measure of the importance attached to bullion an Act of Richard II imposed severe penalties on merchants who were so unpatriotic as to export gold and silver: 'For the great mischief which this realm suffereth and long hath done, that gold and silver are carried out of the realm, so that in effect there is none left thereof, which thing if it should longer be suffered would shortly be the destruction of the same realm, which God prohibit.'

The bullionist tradition continued into the sixteenth and seventeenth centuries when the prophets of economic nationalism were known as mercantilists. They understood the principles of trade

3

to the extent of admitting that it was desirable for the country to receive commodities from abroad, especially those goods that could not easily be produced at home, but they insisted that total exports should always be greater than total imports and the balance should be paid in gold and silver. The result of this policy was an elaborate system of tariff controls to restrict the entry of foreign products.

A tariff is a charge the Government makes on goods coming into the country. It varies from one import to another according to the current economic policy, but occasionally it can be steep enough to make it impossible for a trader to recover the cost of the tariff when he comes to sell his goods. His prices are so high no one is interested in buying.

The principles of mercantilism appealed to the king's ministers who regarded import duties as a useful source of revenue, and attracted the support of powerful groups of traders who enjoyed protection from foreign competitors. Sometimes the merchants did even better by securing extra special concessions. The cloth manufacturers in Elizabeth's reign were able to prohibit the export of wool to keep down the cost of their raw material. The poor consumer seldom benefited, except indirectly, when the export of corn was stopped for strategic reasons which helped to prevent increases in the price of bread.

This hotchpotch of economic ideas remained unquestioned until the mid-eighteenth century, when commerce was preparing for its burst of expansion known as the Industrial Revolution. The new and energetic breed of businessmen objected to the incredible variety of trade restrictions. Their distaste for government meddling found expression in the writings of Adam Smith, a Scottish academic who published, in 1776, his two-volume book, *An Inquiry into the Nature and Causes of the Wealth of Nations*. His proposals were the first clear sign that one day economics would mature into a science but, at the time, they were regarded by his learned colleagues as little short of heresy. He argued that the accumulation of gold and silver was not the principal, much less the sole, purpose of foreign trade.

Between whatever places foreign trade is carried out [he wrote] they all of them derive two distinct benefits from it. It carries out that surplus part of the produce of their land and labour for which there is no demand among them, and brings back in return for it something else for which there is a demand. It gives

4

a value to their superfluities by exchanging them for something else, which may satisfy a part of their wants and increase their enjoyments (**62**).

He called for an end to mercantilism and the tariff system so that men could freely produce and sell the commodities they were best able to produce and sell.

As an illustration of his ideas imagine two islands, one ideally suited to growing coconuts, the other, bananas. Traders on both islands can exchange products and the consumers, who are in a position to buy coconuts and bananas, get the best of both worlds. But supposing the second island decides to stop the importation of coconuts in order to foster a home-based coconut industry. Resources are transferred from the banana business, in which the island does well, to coconuts, a commercial project that takes no account of local conditions. Result—the quality of coconuts declines, the price goes up and the consumers are worse off. Meanwhile, the people on the first island can no longer afford to buy bananas because they are unable to sell their coconuts, so their standard of living declines.

Adam Smith claimed that this type of situation had developed, on a much larger scale, in Britain and the countries with whom she traded. The Government was so intent on cutting down imports that we were being forced to produce at home goods that were much cheaper to buy abroad. Other countries suffered a loss of income and could not afford to purchase all the commodities that Britain was ready to export. Thus the standard of living was unnecessarily depressed all round.

One of the most attractive features of Adam Smith's philosophy was his concern for people—'the welfare of individuals and homes'. If trade did not contribute to the wealth and comfort of the population it was not worth pursuing. This assumption is fundamental to our way of thinking, but in an age when the common people were taught to expect no more than a subsistence living the concept was revolutionary.

The publication of *Wealth of Nations* coincided with the appearance of Jeremy Bentham's *Fragment of Government*, which questioned the political assumptions of mercantilism. Bentham believed that one man's happiness should count for as much as another's and that every man is the best judge of his own interests. Basically, these were the principles of Adam Smith and though neither he nor Bentham were immediately acclaimed their ideas—transformed into the theory of laissez faire, or minimum government interference in the national economic order—were to dominate administrative thinking in the nineteenth century. Meanwhile, the French Revolution and the American Declaration of Independence gave a strong impetus to their brand of individualism.

2 The End of the Corn Laws

One of the earliest influential converts to free trade was William Pitt who, in 1783—at the early age of twenty-four—was appointed Prime Minister and Chancellor of the Exchequer. He believed that Adam Smith had given to the world the best solution to all commercial and economic questions. On one occasion his hero remarked that Pitt seemed to understand his ideas better than he understood them himself.

Even so he approached the job of dismantling the tariff barriers with extreme caution. Mercantilism had its powerful defenders and import duties were an important source of revenue that could not be abandoned overnight. The first task was to reorganise the system. There was certainly room for improvement. Customs theoretically brought in £700,000 a year, but smuggling was so widespread that the Exchequer was lucky if it received a third of that sum. For instance, a fantastic duty of 119 per cent was imposed on tea so it was not surprising that of the 13 million lb yearly consumption, almost two-thirds were shipped in illegally. Importers who preferred honest dealings often found they were expected to make not one but several payments on items purchased abroad. One commentator noted: 'What a maze our merchants must be in. . . . Can we wonder at the decay of our commerce? . . . Should we not wonder that we have any left?'

Pitt substituted one rate for the various duties charged on each article. Then he reduced the tariff on a wide range of imports (on tea it was lowered to 12½ per cent) and tightened up the laws against smuggling by his Hovering Act which empowered officials to search vessels up to four leagues out to sea.

The process of breaking down the trade restrictions was brought to a sudden end by the outbreak of war against France in 1793. One of the setbacks of this period was the failure of the Pitt–Vergennes treaty with France by which both countries had agreed to a freer exchange of commodities. A proposal to abolish the limitations on trade between Britain and Ireland also foundered, this time because manufacturers were persuaded that Irish competition would endanger their profits. Finally, despite Pitt's efforts, there were still 1,500 different rates of customs duties, and nearly every home-produced article was protected in some way. It became clear to the reformers that the route to free trade was a long, slow haul.

The Treaty of Vienna, signed in 1815, was followed by industrial depression and political unrest as the country painfully readapted itself to a peacetime economy. But by 1820 trade was building up to another boom period that was to establish Britain as the greatest commercial nation in the world. The first postwar move against protection was inspired by the merchants of London who complained to Parliament of the 'impolicy and injustice of the restriction system' and appealed for duty-free imports. They were supported by the Edinburgh Chamber of Commerce and those industrialists who were eager to obtain cheap raw materials. The House of Commons was sympathetic, but the Prime Minister, Lord Liverpool, put his finger on the central problem when he replied, '. . . the difficulty of the reform of taxation is in the vested interests which have grown up and which could be imperilled if any attempt is made at such a design' (**10**).

The President of the Board of Trade was William Huskisson, a politician whose attitude to commerce was entirely conditioned by the theories of Adam Smith. Like the Prime Minister he realised the strength of the opposition and his speeches were sometimes tougher than his actions. Of the silk business he said: 'We are far behind other nations in this industry, it [protection] has a chilling and benumbing effect, men are rendered indifferent to exertion by the indolent security of the prohibitory system.' He then reduced the import duty on raw silk from $4d$ to $1d$ per lb, and on thrown silk from $14s$ $8d$ to $5s$ per lb which sounded courageous but was unopposed since the cost of raw material was correspondingly lowered. Manufactured silk previously prohibited, was admitted at a duty of 30 per cent, enough to give ample protection. Yet there was a painful outcry from the industry, whose representatives claimed they would be ruined by their French competitors.

Huskisson succeeded in lowering duties on a variety of raw materials including flax, iron, copper, lead and zinc. He lifted the embargo on the export of wool and aimed at a tariff on manufactured imports not exceeding 30 per cent. With a strong industry like cotton which had no foreign rivals he cut duties ranging from 50 to 75 per cent to a uniform 10 per cent. He achieved Pitt's ambition to abolish restrictions on trade between Britain and Ireland, liberalised the Navigation Acts, which were originally designed to give British ships a monopoly of carrying foreign goods to home ports, and continued the work of simplifying the administrative machine. When he retired from politics and life (he was run over and fatally injured by Stephenson's *Rocket* at the opening of the Manchester to Liverpool railway in 1830) the number of Acts of Parliament regulating customs had been reduced from nearly 1,500 to 11. But there were still over 1,000 different rates of duty and he had taken no action against the landowners, the strongest vested interest involved in the struggle to keep protection (**20**).

Agriculture was by no means a declining or bankrupt industry, but it suffered market fluctuations that were not experienced in other trades. Then, as now, the farmers' ideal harvest was not too much and not too little. An exceptionally good crop caused a glut of produce and low prices, while an exceptionally bad harvest raised prices only for those farmers lucky enough to have anything to sell. It seemed only reasonable that men who earned their living at such a risky and essential occupation should not have the additional worry of competing with foreign rivals. If there was any doubt in the matter the landed gentry could rely on a sympathetic hearing from Parliament, where they held a dominant influence.

But their power did not extend to the manufacturing regions of the North where the new industrialists were more interested in cheap food for their workers than in the welfare of the agricultural community. They pointed out that the population had increased by more than three times between 1750 and 1821 when it was over 21 million. Britain was no longer a country that could survive on home-grown food.

Especially important was the supply of corn, which provided the basic diet for the vast majority of the people. During the Napoleonic War, when imports were held up by enemy action, the price of corn rose from 43*s* a quarter to a maximum of 126*s* and the landowners were happy. But the consumers were naturally less cheerful and expected a better deal when the fighting came to an end. Instead,

9

Parliament revived a regulation, known as the Corn Law, by which the importation of foreign wheat was prohibited until the price of home grown wheat exceeded a certain price—in this case, 80s per quarter. There were similar restrictions on barley and oats.

The system had the advantage of simplicity but it was totally ineffective in achieving its purpose. Disappointing harvests in 1816 and 1817 raised wheat prices to an average of 96s 11d a quarter and there was a desperate food shortage. Theoretically, foreign merchants should have taken immediate advantage of the opportunity to sell their corn on the British market but they could not be expected to guess some time ahead that their services would be required and they needed time to make the necessary arrangements. Eventually when large quantities of imported wheat and flour arrived at the docks, chiefly from Russia, Poland and Prussia, it was too late to prevent starvation among the poorest families.

Even the farmers were not satisfied. Most of them were tenants of wealthy landowners who increased their rents in the expectation that the Corn Law would lead to higher profits. But Government regulations did not prevent a catastrophic fall in prices when the harvest was above average and on these occasions the situation was aggravated by the supply of foreign wheat which usually reached its highest point at the end of a bad season.

Parliament could think of no solution that would satisfy both producers and consumers. The normal compromise was to modify the existing legislation in favour of those who protested with the loudest voice. In 1822 the Government decided to allow imports after the price of wheat had risen to 70s—a reduction of 10s on the 1815 figure. Six years later the Government led by the Duke of Wellington, of which Huskisson and Sir Robert Peel were members, approved a more elaborate and ambitious Corn Law. It took the form of a sliding scale based on a standard level of 64s. At that price a duty of 23s 8d was imposed on foreign corn and the tariff scale was gradually reduced as the price increased, so that at 73s the duty was only 1s per quarter.

The originators of this scheme earned no applause from the people they were trying to help. Industrialists and workers in the towns constantly complained that bread was too expensive, while the farmers bitterly reminded their landlords that prices were fluctuating as wildly as in any period they could remember. There was increasing sympathy among the administrators for the views of the 1821 Parliamentary Committee on agricultural distress, whose members expressed 'a doubt whether the only solid foundation of the flourishing state of agriculture is not laid in abstaining as much as possible from interference either by Protection or Prohibition with the application of capital in any branch of industry'.

The Parliamentary Reform Bill of 1832 which enfranchised the urban middle class strengthened the confidence of the Corn Law abolitionists who saw clearly that the landed interest was losing its monopoly of political power. On the other hand, from 1832 to 1836 the country was prosperous and public agitation against the Corn Laws lacked the urgency that low wages and food shortages were bound to stimulate. Parliamentary resolutions supporting the free importation of corn were hotly opposed and overwhelmingly defeated.

'During my long life,' said Lord Melbourne, the aristocratic Whig Prime Minister who came to office in 1834, 'it has been my lot to hear many mad things proposed, but the maddest of all mad things to which I have ever had to listen is the proposal to abolish the Corn Laws.'

Towards the end of 1836 the economic climate changed abruptly. A bad harvest was followed by an industrial depression, a drop in the level of wages and heavy unemployment. At the same time the effects of the 1834 Poor Law Amendment Act provided another cause of working-class antagonism. Instead of receiving financial relief paupers were forced to go into workhouses, where they lived in cruel and degrading servitude (**20**).

In September 1838, when the price of wheat had risen to 77*s* and seven to eight million people were without bread, a few enthusiastic free traders in Manchester agreed to set up an Anti-Corn Law Association. A provisional committee of thirty-eight members was advertised, and among them was John Bright. A week later the name of Richard Cobden was added to the list. Their partnership was to become synonymous with the campaign to demolish the tariff barriers. Both were self-made and successful business men who believed that protection in general, and the Corn Laws in particular, were holding up the progress of British industry. They were idealists who looked to a time when worldwide free trade could bring international peace and security founded on enlightened self-interest (**58**).

In March 1839 the Association was formed into a national organisation called the Anti-Corn Law League. For the next seven years a barrage of propaganda was directed at the public. Pamph-

lets were distributed, lectures presented and a paper called simply
The League achieved a wide circulation (**49**).

Meetings were rowdy and often violent, especially when League
speakers were barracked by Chartists. These campaigners took
their name from the Charter on which their proposed reforms were
based and prescribed universal suffrage as the first step to solving
the problem of working-class distress. They were prepared, even
enthusiastic, to abolish the Corn Laws as part of a wider programme
when they attained power, but they were convinced that the middle-
class Leaguers were motivated more by a desire to make life easier
for the manufacturers who could use the excuse of cheap bread to
lower wages, than by a sympathy with the poorer sections of the
community [**docs 1 and 2**].

But turbulent or not, the Anti-Corn Law assemblies were so
successful that in Manchester no hall was large enough to cater for
all those who wished to attend and Cobden provided a site in St
Peter's Field, on which the Free-trade Hall was built. This was the
spot where Henry Hunt's political reform meeting was broken up
by troops in 1819, an incident that became known as the Peterloo
massacre. Now, in 1843, it was the scene of gigantic demonstrations
appealing for cheap bread [**doc. 3**].

The League was 'non-political' in the sense that it attacked the
landed interest in the Whig and Tory parties. Its leading supporters
included genuine humanitarians who wanted to make life easier
for the poor, free-traders who sought the removal of all restraints
on trade, and self-interested employers who associated cheap bread
with cheap labour. They were united by a single purpose and their
determination was like a religious mania. They sought converts in
every part of the country and every sector of the community.
Disciples were even sent into the rural areas where farmers were
told that high rents were the result of inflated corn prices. Few were
convinced. With the help of the Penny Post, inaugurated in 1840,
millions of leaflets were sent to the unenfranchised urban workers
who represented a potentially powerful body of agitators (**31**).

On the surface Parliament was unimpressed by all this activity,
and Lord Melbourne told a deputation from the League that 'repeal
was impracticable'. But privately he was less confident, and when
one of his ministers showed him a speech he intended making on the
Corn Laws, Melbourne advised him to tone it down: 'It is reproval
and condemnation, and there is in it a good deal of sarcasm. The

middle and lower orders are very touchy and, above all things, hate to be sneered at.'

Within a year the Chancellor of the Exchequer, Lord John Russell, proposed in his budget speech a scheme to replace the sliding scale by a moderate fixed duty of 8*s* per quarter on wheat, 4*s* 6*d* on barley and 3*s* 6*d* on oats, and to modify the duties on sugar and timber. The aim, paradoxically, was not to satisfy the free traders but to solve the Government's financial problems. For example, the existing customs regulations for timber stipulated that imports from the Baltic paid a prohibitive duty, while Canadian timber was allowed in at a much lower rate. Russell proposed lowering the foreign duty and raising the Canadian duty, thus allowing for a greater volume of imports and increased Government revenue. Similarly there was a heavy colonial preference on sugar which gave the West Indian producers a virtual monopoly. Russell wanted a lower rate on foreign sugar which could then compete in the British market. The new corn duties would also raise additional money for the Exchequer by encouraging higher imports.

The free-traders were in need of a morale booster and they were delighted with Russell's performance, whatever his motives. But they reckoned without the vested interests whose representatives on both sides of the House of Commons combined to defeat the Government. At the subsequent general election the Conservatives won a majority and Sir Robert Peel became Prime Minister. Richard Cobden was elected for Stockport. He lost no time in declaring his allegiance. 'I call myself neither Whig nor Tory,' he said, 'I am a Free Trader.' In 1843 he was joined by John Bright, member for Durham.

This was the period when the Anti-Corn Law campaign centred on Parliament and, as if to emphasise the change in tactics, the League's headquarters was moved from Manchester to London. Cobden was positive that success was 'merely a question of time'. He was not above using the customary practices of intimidation and bribery to achieve a victory at the hustings, but he resisted the demands of John Bright and the militants who at one point advocated closing the factories as a method of forcing the government's hand (**49, 58**).

He had valid cause to be self-confident. The social and political power of the urban middle class was growing and would continue to grow, while the landowners were nervously aware of their weak defensive position. More important, Peel was a convert to free trade,

13

and, though leader of a party in which the agricultural pressure group held the largest block of votes, he was prepared to risk dissension for the sake of what he now regarded as a healthy commercial policy. As a start he adapted the trade proposals of the Whig Government, modified the sliding scale on corn, and lowered duties on a wide selection of manufactured goods and raw materials. By including timber but excluding sugar from his tariff amendments he split his opponents and gained majority support for a long jump towards free trade. At the same time he boosted Exchequer revenue by imposing an income tax of $7d$ in the £.

Cobden and his associates were encouraged to step up their campaign in the country and in Parliament. They could not reasonably expect the Prime Minister to agree immediately to their demands (his following in the Commons was insecure and the military implications of a greater reliance on foreign corn worried him), but they anticipated that popular demand would help him to resolve his fears. Plans were made to increase the number of League candidates at the next election, and uncommitted members were lobbied by their free-trade colleagues, who used every argument statistics could provide to win their allegiance.

Cobden and Bright led a formidable parliamentary debating team but they were painfully aware that weeks and months of discussion were worth not half so much as a really bad harvest. It came in 1845 and turned out to be a more powerful weapon than even the League could have expected. Heavy rain took the wheat farmers by surprise and, simultaneously, a potato blight wiped out the autumn crop of Ireland's staple food.

Starvation in Ireland and a sudden rise in the home price of bread stimulated fierce opposition to the Corn Laws. Lord John Russell, who had taken over from Melbourne as leader of the Whig Party, dramatically announced his conversion to free trade and called for 'an end to a system which had been proved to be the blight of commerce, the bane of agriculture, the source of bitter divisions among classes, the cause of penury, fever, mortality and crime among the people' (**49**).

This was the crisis Cobden had been waiting for. League membership increased with every fresh report of suffering at home and in Ireland. Ironically, the Government made the food shortage in Ireland worse than it might have been by following, to some extent, the principles of Adam Smith and the free-traders. At the height of the famine Irish wheat was allowed to leave the country to satisfy the demands of the English market. Officials shuddered at the thought of interfering in the process of legitimate commerce.

Cobden's solution to this economic paradox was to permit the unrestricted entry of foreign corn. Free imports would bring cheap bread, he argued, and the Prime Minister expressed his agreement, though both politicians realised that given the harvest conditions abroad and the transport problems, there was no possibility of an immediate heavy influx of foreign corn. In any case, multitudes of Irish peasants were so poor after the loss of their potato crop they could not afford to buy a single loaf however low its price. But the crisis provided an ideal excuse for implementing a policy that would in the opinion of its supporters, bring long-term benefits. Peel suggested to his ministers the suspension of the Corn Laws. Most of them were persuaded to follow his lead, but he refused to act without unanimous support from the Cabinet and resigned. Lord John Russell attempted to form a government, but the divisions within his own party on matters other than free trade were such that he gave up the effort and the responsibility was passed back to Sir John Peel, who now realised that he was the only leader in a position to carry through the necessary legislation.

Having reassembled his administration he decided that if he was going to antagonise the old guard he might as well do the job properly. He produced a neat package deal which included the repeal of almost all duties on raw materials. The restrictions on corn were to be reduced gradually until they were abolished in 1849 (hardly a crisis measure) and from that time on the only tax on corn was to be a revenue duty of 1*s* per quarter (**44**).

A majority of MPs accepted the proposals either as an expression of loyalty to Peel or because of their genuine sympathy for free trade. Even so, two-thirds of the Tory members voted against the Prime Minister. His party was split and his political career ruined by the landowners, who saw him as the betrayer of their interests [**doc. 4**]. A few days after the Bill was passed Cobden spoke in the Manchester Free-trade Hall: 'If he [Peel] has lost office, he has gained a country. For my part, I would rather descend to private life with that last measure of his . . . than mount to the highest pinnacle of human power by any other means.'

At the end of the meeting the Anti-Corn Law League was quietly dissolved.

15

Part Two

PROTECTION

3 The Nineteenth-century Revival

The abolition of the Corn Laws did not have the disastrous effect on agriculture that the landowners had prophesied. Wheat prices dropped but only slightly and those politicians, including Peel, who guessed that the problems of rapid bulk transport over long distances would normally deter foreign countries from exporting vast quantities of corn, were proved correct. Yet the general public was not disappointed. For one thing, free trade prevented abnormally high prices, since there was usually just enough foreign corn available to keep the market steady, even when the home harvest was bad. More important, Britain was entering a phase of industrial prosperity for which a number of factors, including free trade, were responsible. Mechanisation raised output, the railway revolution speeded up the delivery of raw materials and finished products, while the discovery of gold in California and Australia in the late 1840s brought unexpected additional wealth to those areas which led to a bonus demand for British goods. Naturally, the standard of living improved along with the growth of national wealth, and the unsophisticated consumers, who knew nothing of economics except what Cobden and his friends had taught them in their speeches and literature, assumed that free trade was solely responsible for their good fortune.

In these circumstances the protectionists could not hope for a reversal of trade policy and though Lord George Bentinck and Disraeli led a Conservative campaign for the restoration of the Corn Laws (Disraeli's attack on Peel established him as a candidate for high office in any future Conservative government) they were soon forced to admit that a return to the old system was out of the question (**15**). During the next few years the remaining tariff barriers were marked out for demolition. In 1853 when Gladstone was Chancellor of the Exchequer, in a Liberal Government whose members already regarded themselves as the trustees of free trade, the duties on 123 articles were abolished and those on 133 reduced.

Protection

This was part of his effort 'to bring to completion the noble work of commercial reform', an ambition that by 1860 had led him to reduce the tariff list to a mere forty-eight articles. In that year the Anglo-French Treaty, inspired and negotiated by Richard Cobden, was finally ratified. For her part, Britain agreed to abolish all duties on manufactured goods, reduce the duty on brandy and adopt a lower scale on the importation of wines—concessions that were offered to all countries but were chiefly applicable to France. In return French duties were lowered on a range of imports from Britain; other countries continued to pay the higher tariff rates. Ironically, the agreement was later used by the protectionists as an argument for erecting new tariffs. Britain had made a good bargain by winning favoured nation treatment from France, but similar treaties with other countries were impossible since free-trade Britain now had nothing to offer. Import duties, said the protectionists, were useful weapons for those engaged in international commerce—Cobden, the complete free-trader had proved that. His defenders claimed that the problem would be answered when other nations followed Britain's example and removed their customs barriers—but this they resolutely refused to do.

What was more important, Germany, France and the United States took advantage of protection to build up their own powerful industrial economies, and by the late 1870s they were ready to compete for the export markets on equal terms. Britain was no longer the sole 'workshop of the world', as her businessmen discovered to their shocked surprise when they lost valuable orders to their American and continental rivals. And this at a time when prices and profits were dropping largely as a result of lower costs and increased output. They might have reacted with better humour if these same rivals had not excluded many British goods from their home markets by imposing high import duties. If that's the game they want to play, said the free-trade critics, why can't we abide by same rules?

The back-to-protection call was echoed by some landowners and farmers who were worried by the growing food imports. Larger and faster merchant vessels were overcoming the problem of distance that Peel had relied on to cushion agriculture against foreign competition. In the 1870s there were no less than five disastrous harvests, but prices remained low because the deficiency of corn was made up by supplies from abroad.

The revival of interest in protection was marked by the birth of the Fair Trade League led by Farrer Ecroyd, the head of a large worsted firm and MP for Preston from 1881 (**19**). The chief sponsors of the organisation were wealthy and exclusively Conservative industrialists, who believed that falling prices and profits meant they were in the middle of a serious depression. They advocated moderate duties on imported manufactured goods and agricultural produce as a remedy for their attack of economic jitters.

At the same time a cross section of Conservative constituency associations passed resolutions in favour of protection, but, with the 1885 election on hand, support from the leadership seldom went beyond a mild expression of regret that Britain was unable to retaliate against foreign tariffs. The 'hungry 'forties' were not forgotten and while free trade was associated with cheap bread, protection was not likely to win many votes. After the Conservative victory the Prime Minister, Lord Salisbury, set up a Royal Commission to inquire into the causes of the unfavourable economic trends. This resulted in a minority report which expressed approval for the principles of 'fair trade'.

In 1887 the annual Conservative Conference passed by a massive majority a resolution in favour of a general tariff, and for a time it was at least conceivable that the fair traders would either cause a split in the party or force some sort of compromise policy on the leadership. In 1890 a temporary revival in trade put fresh heart into the free-traders and the pressure on the Government was correspondingly lessened.

Meanwhile the idea of imperialism was beginning to take a hold in the country. The British Empire was the most gigantic collection of territories which had ever in the history of the world been brought under a single political system, and yet, until the 1870s, the mother country attached little value to it, and since its English-speaking members had almost complete self-government, there was a vague assumption that sooner or later the various units would break away and become independent states. Even Disraeli in his early political career regarded the colonies as 'millstones round our neck', but when he became Prime Minister he gave the country a new sense of pride by emphasising the commercial and strategic importance of British imperial interests. The Suez Canal was secured, Victoria became Empress of India, and between 1878 and 1879 the Transvaal was annexed and Afghanistan, unhappily required for the north-western defence of India, was invaded. Both expeditions were noted for their military and political incompetence (**15**).

There followed a Gladstonian interlude (1880–86) when the Government was less attracted to the idea of colonial expansion and the Transvaal and Afghanistan were abandoned. But an attempt to give Ireland back to the Irish was defeated by Joe Chamberlain and his followers, who deserted the Liberal Party and crossed the House to the Conservative benches. As Prime Minister, Lord Salisbury followed the now established Tory tradition and engaged in a vigorous imperial policy. Firmly backed by party opinion, he threw himself wholeheartedly into a struggle for possessions, chiefly in Africa, which was to end in the acquisition for the British Empire of some six million square miles of territory (**43**).

The growth of imperial sentiment at home and nationalism in Europe, where the process of unification was at work in Italy and Germany, led statesmen and political writers to think about the need for establishing closer links between the mother country and the older and self-governing members of the Empire—Canada, Australia and New Zealand. In 1884 the Imperial Federation League was founded with the support of Lord Rosebery and W. E. Forster, author of the 1870 Education Act.

The colonial spokesmen were cautious. Quite reasonably, they were only interested in an offer which would appeal to their own electorates. They were not taken in by the patronising approach and it seemed difficult for British statesmen to rid themselves of the illusion that colonials were humble subjects whose sole aspiration was to receive friendly recognition from the home country.

Most of the ambitious schemes discussed at this time shared the defect of emphasising the subordinate role which the colonies would assume in a united Empire. For example, the Government might be expanded so as to admit one delegate from each colony, or the colonies might relinquish their legislatures and re-attach themselves to an augmented House of Commons (**51**). But Canada, Australia and New Zealand were already acquiring their own sense of nationality and independence. They did not intend to submit themselves to what they regarded as 'Westminster domination'.

In 1887 imperial delegates gathered in London to celebrate the fiftieth anniversary of Queen Victoria's accession to the throne. The occasion provided an ideal opportunity to meet in conference to discuss matters of common interest including defence, inter-imperial communications and trade. It soon became clear that the colonies were willing to consider arrangements for the expansion of Empire commerce. Whether from genuine concern for the political future of Britain and the Empire, or merely with an eye to the main chance, the protectionists snatched eagerly at the opportunity for advertising their own views. In 1891 the Fair Trade League was succeeded by the United Empire Trade League. The founder members were Howard Vincent and James Lowther, two Conservative Members of Parliament who were active protectionists. They evolved a plan for a self-supporting Empire, voluntarily bound together by an interlocking system of trade. The basic idea was to impose a tariff on all imports except raw materials, and to negotiate reciprocal preferential concessions with the colonies. For practical purposes the question of preferential trading was limited to Canada, Australia and New Zealand, since the other members of the Empire had no protective tariffs of any importance. But the hope of establishing a closer relationship with these young and potentially powerful nations which would lead eventually to Empire unity was calculated to bring about a revolutionary change in British fiscal policy (**41**).

Unfortunately for the League there were divergent views in the self-governing colonies and the mother country on the nature of a customs arrangement. From the British point of view the ideal scheme was not imperial preference but a customs union with free trade within the Empire and protection against the foreigner. If the proposal had been acceptable to the self-governing colonies, many a British free-trader would have sacrificed his economic principles for the cause. Indeed, the exponents could pose as the only true free-traders. Peace and cooperation secured by, and in the interests of, trade was a good Cobdenite principle and, while its application within the scope of the Empire was at least feasible, the orthodox free-traders were bound to admit that as far as Europe and America were concerned it was a non-starter.

For good reasons colonial opinion favoured the policy advocated by the United Empire Trade League. Free trade with Britain would involve the loss of a high proposition of the national revenues since tariffs were regarded as a legitimate means of spreading the load of taxation over all classes of the community. More important, the self-governing colonies were still in the early stages of industrialisation, and growth could be seriously impeded by competition on equal terms with British products. Manufacturers could not be blamed if they interpreted the 'Empire Unity' theme as a thinly disguised attempt on the part of the British to reimpose the old colonial economic pattern—the exchange of agricultural produce and raw material for English industrial goods. The self-governing colonies wished to be treated as equals, not as inferior partners whose sole function was to feed the people and the factories of the mother country.

If Britain adopted a general tariff with Empire preference the colonies could respond by lowering, but not abandoning, their duties on British imports. Thus an adequate tariff revenue would be secured, satisfactory protection for the infant industries maintained, and a wider British market for colonial products guaranteed. The vital question was whether Britain was prepared to take the risk of abandoning free trade. In the short run the answer was an unequivocal 'no'. The bait was simply not big enough.

The position was made perfectly clear as a result of the discussions at the Intercolonial Conference which met at Ottawa in 1894. While delegates argued in support of preferential tariffs, the British representative pointed out that about 75 per cent of Britain's export and import trade was still with foreign countries and of the remainder only half was with Australia, New Zealand and Canada. What was more the proportion of colonial to foreign trade had barely changed since 1854. In other words, Britain was being asked to impose high tariffs on most of her imports for the sake of a concession on the minority of her goods exported to the self-governing colonies. It was precisely this fact which attracted the United Empire Trade League to the scheme.

They realised that imperial preference was bound to offer the British manufacturer almost complete protection. But the free-traders were naturally appalled by the suggestion even if it did hold out some hope of Empire unity. Their favourite argument was to remind the public that imperial preference would bring food taxation. A very high proportion of Britain's food imports came from foreign countries and while the agriculturalist, whose aim was to arrest the declining fortunes of his industry, was delighted by the prospects of a scheme which offered complete protection from a major group of competitors, the consumers were less attracted to the proposition. The possibility of higher prices for foreign wheat revived the 'dear loaf' scare, and made the protectionist pill virtually unacceptable for the less affluent sector of the community.

For a time the United Empire League was able to acquire serious attention at least from those Conservatives to whom loyalty to the Empire had become the first test of patriotism, but they were treated with less respect by the Liberals for whom free trade was the foundation stone of their economic doctrine and by leading Conservative politicians who had other factors to take into account—including the voting intentions of the electorate. After the return of the Liberals in 1892 the House of Commons was preoccupied with the Irish question. Gladstone had the satisfaction of seeing his second Home Rule Bill passed by the House of Commons and the humiliation of witnessing its destruction in the House of Lords. He retired in disgust and the leadership passed to Lord Rosebery. The Tories felt strong enough to follow up on their victory and the Liberals stood by while the rest of their programme was mutilated by a hostile majority in the Lords. An election could not be postponed for very long and the Opposition, which calculated that the mere ineffectiveness of the Liberal Government would ensure the return to power of the Conservatives, promised little and avoided issues which might put them on the defensive.

Certainly it was no time to dabble with protection, and Salisbury, who on more than one occasion had hinted that Britain might be forced to resort to retaliatory measures against foreign tariffs, replied to a correspondent regretting that there was no likelihood 'of the question of protection being favourably considered in the coming parliamentary sessions, or, indeed, in any session which it is possible at present to foresee'.

In the House of Commons two leading personalities in the United Empire Trade League kept themselves in the news by attacking on a broad front and by offering a possible remedy for the economic grievances of various pressure groups. Both of them supported Empire preference, as the only possible remedy for Britain's trade problems. The Rt. Hon. James Lowther had, in the past, held ministerial rank, as Under-Secretary of State for the Colonies and Chief Secretary for Ireland. He became well known as a protectionist and as the regular mover of the rejection of the Sessional Order against the interference of peers in parliamentary elections. Lowther was regarded by his parliamentary colleagues as something of a character. Everyone knew him as 'Jimmy' Lowther, a great sportsman and racing enthusiast, entertaining and harmless.

A more forceful personality was Howard Vincent, Conservative member for Central Sheffield since 1885 (**41**). Dogged all his life by a consumptive cough and a weak heart, he nevertheless succeeded in marking out for himself a varied career. He spent the early years of his working life as an army officer, a law student, and a journalist on military affairs. In 1878 he was appointed Director of Criminal Investigations at Scotland Yard. When, after another six years he finally determined to enter politics, his first inclination was to put himself forward as a candidate in the Liberal interest. A world tour which took him to most of the countries of the Empire converted him to Tory imperialism and on his return he was adopted as Conservative candidate for the Sheffield constituency which he was to represent until his death in 1908.

Most of Vincent's political career was devoted to the cause of protection and Empire preference. Over the years he built up a considerable influence among the rank and file of the Tory Party. He was one of the chief speakers for the protectionist motion which was passed by the annual conference in 1887. Eight years later he was Chairman of the Party Conference. If the House of Commons was less inclined to take him seriously, his ability to dream up awkward questions for the President of the Board of Trade and his single-minded persistence in snatching at every opportunity to propagate his views earned him the affection of his colleagues and opponents. He was one who 'adds to the gaiety of the House'. Only *The Times* found him irritating and described him sarcastically as the member who 'can scarcely conceive of English commerce enjoying real prosperity without some fostering care on his part'.

The protectionists had one certain ally in the Conservative Government. Henry Chaplin was elected member for the Sleaford Division in 1868, a seat which he held until the 1906 election (**47**). From his early days in politics he subscribed to protection as a cure for agricultural ills. The problems of industry and the question of Empire unity were of marginal interest to him. In 1881 he joined in the by-election fight in North Lincolnshire in support of Lowther who had lost his seat in the general election. From the platform, Chaplin and Lowther preached the gospel of fair trade. When 'the Squire' took office as President of the Local Government Board in the 1895 Government his colleagues did not expect him to recant his economic opinions but they could not permit him to propagate them in his ministerial capacity. It was clear that Chaplin was not available for active participation in the protectionist campaign but, for those who were bearing the brunt of the work, it was a comfort to have the moral support of a member of the Cabinet.

Among the MPs and candidates in the Tory Party who fought the 1895 election, there was a tough contingent of protectionists, whose sentiments ranged from a simple desire to 'strengthen our links with the colonies', to the demand for a full-scale review of fiscal policy with the purpose of introducing a general tariff. But the leadership remained solidly free trade. The Campaign Guide offered no encouragement even to those whose first aim was to achieve a working arrangement with the colonies. The authors expressed enthusiasm for the conception of Empire unity, but dismissed a customs arrangement as 'impracticable', pinning their faith on the Imperial Federation League project for Dominion representatives in London, greater cooperation on defence and organised emigration. The objective was political union. It was a forlorn hope, and it is perhaps significant that even though its plan survived, the Imperial Federation League was dissolved in 1894, leaving many of its members, including Rosebery, thoroughly disillusioned.

For the time being protection and preference were politically taboo, but the future was promising. Salisbury unconsciously reinforced the small band of campaigners when, having won the election, he brought into the Government a man whose status and popularity was soon to be their best hope of success. He invited Joseph Chamberlain to become Colonial Secretary.

4 Joe Chamberlain

Ambitious and egoistic, with an inexhaustible capacity for hard political campaigning, Chamberlain abandoned a successful business career at the age of forty and devoted himself to the municipal affairs of Birmingham—he was elected Mayor in 1873—and to politics. In 1876 he carried his famous monocle to the House of Commons, where the new Birmingham member firmly allied himself to the radical wing of the Liberal Party and absorbed himself in the fight for social reform. The fiscal question was not, during this period, a burning political topic and it is hardly surprising that as a radical and a disciple of John Bright, another Birmingham representative, his occasional utterances on the subject should reveal him as an orthodox free-trader who was not prepared to squander the resources of his country in colonial expansion. On the other hand, while supporting concessions to the Irish, he was, from the start, an opponent of Home Rule, believing that it would seriously weaken Britain in times of emergency to have an independent country so close to her shores.

But the significant fact in Chamberlain's early political career was his tendency to take an independent line. To him 'party discipline' and 'party policy' were meaningless phrases and he used the political machine which he was painstakingly constructing in Birmingham not in the Liberal interest as such but in the furtherance of his own schemes.

Irish Home Rule was the paramount issue in the 1885 election and though Chamberlain was prepared to accept local self-government for Ireland, the Gladstonian plan spelt 'separation' and he resigned from the Government a few weeks after its formation. He was out on a limb, forced into an unnatural alliance with the Whig section of the Liberal Party who were just as conservative as the Conservatives and who joined him in the opposition against Home Rule.

Salisbury succeeded in employing his energy usefully by getting Chamberlain to represent Britain on a Commission formed to settle with the USA an age-old fisheries dispute. The job offered opportunities of travel in Canada and America, and his speeches reveal a growing consciousness of the possibilities of Empire development. Already, during the Home Rule battle, he had applied his thoughts to grandiose schemes of Empire unity. 'I hope we may be able sooner or later to federate, to bring together all these great independencies of the British Empire into one supreme and Imperial Parliament, so that they should all be units on one body' (**17**).

The prospect of losing Ireland had concentrated his attention upon the inherent weaknesses of an Empire held together only by ties of sentiment. The movement towards self-government had been allowed to advance without thought for Britain's strength or security: '. . . these colonies are connected with us by ties which are really very loose' he said, 'and if we get into a war . . . they would break adrift and become separate countries' (**17**).

He was quick to catch on to a popular theme and to identify himself as a sympathiser of the Empire Federalists. He had outgrown the anti-imperial philosophy of John Bright whose views on federation were devastatingly clear [**doc. 5**].

In Toronto (December 1887) he referred to the Canadians and British as 'branches of one family' and expressed the hope that the confederation of Canada 'might be the lamp to light our path to the confederation of the British Empire' (**6**). Later, he spoke enthusiastically of 'the friendship of unbroken amity between Great Britain and the United States', which 'is the best guarantee for the peace and civilisation of the world'. He returned to Britain, his political education having advanced a step. He had become a strong believer in the power of the Anglo-Saxon race and, even more significant, he had confirmed his belief in the immense potentialities of the Empire.

Eighteen-eighty-seven was the year of the first Colonial Conference, and Chamberlain listened with some interest to the suggestions for strengthening the trade links with the colonies. In particular he considered the question of a tariff agreement with Canada, entering into correspondence on the subject with Sir Thomas Farrer, who had recently retired as Permanent Secretary of the Board of Trade. Farrer was a determined free-trader and a rigid opponent of unorthodox theories. His reaction was predictable:

I am satisfied . . . that it would be dangerous and mischievous to connect ourselves by any Tariff bargains with Canada—dangerous to our Free Trade policy; dangerous to the union of the Canadian provinces; dangerous in the end to the unity of the Empire. If they asked us to open our ports it would be one thing. What they want us to do is to close them and to lay the foundations for the reconstruction of the old Colonial system which failed so egregiously. It would be the first step on a downward path (3).

Chamberlain evidently thought that some sacrifice was worthwhile for the sake of a closer relationship with the Canadians but Farrer was adamant: 'I dread and mistrust these Canadian politicians altogether. They will use us as a catspaw if they can' (3). The pressure was effective. Chamberlain agreed that while 'we have to watch for opportunities to strengthen the ties between our colonies and ourselves . . . all we can do is wait until proposals are made to us . . . and to accept them if they do not involve the sacrifice of any important principle' (i.e. free trade).

With Chamberlain's conversion to imperialism, an alliance with the Tories was established in all but name, but for the moment there was no question of merging their identities and Chamberlain's group of Liberal Unionists (reduced to forty-seven MPs in the 1892 election) maintained their own party organisation.

Meanwhile, Chamberlain revised his ideas for improving the living conditions of the working class. He relied increasingly on a policy of imperial expansion and development of the British possessions to increase trade and to provide the work and wages which would help to ameliorate the economic distress. As early as 1893 he was arguing that the remedy for unemployment was not to be found in the establishment of municipal workshops or the limitations of the hours of labour, remedies widely favoured by social reformers, but in the development and extension of Empire markets for British manufacturers. He returned to this theme again and again, on each occasion adding a touch of spice to his proposals by appealing to a wider patriotism. 'We are landlords of a great estate,' he said on one occasion, 'it is the duty of the landlord to develop his estate.'

The 1895 election gave victory to the Tories, and Chamberlain, having turned down an offer to become Secretary for War, accepted the Colonial Office. His first move was to send a circular to the governors of the various colonies requesting them to supply information on the extent to which foreign goods were displacing British products in colonial markets, and the reasons for what appeared to be a changing pattern of trade.

It is unlikely that Chamberlain intended much more than to trace the causes of the successful advance of foreign competition, but some of the protectionists—James Lowther among them—and a number of colonial journalists, chiefly Australian, interpreted his investigation as the first step towards the negotiation of inter-imperial trade agreements based on a general tariff with a concessional rate for colonial imports.

The Empire preference crusaders were not to win the allegiance of the Colonial Secretary quite so easily. So far the only concession which Chamberlain had made to the protectionists was to express his support for Howard Vincent's campaign to prevent the importation into Britain of goods made in prisons abroad. He was certainly considering the possibility of embarking on trade negotiations, but his inclination was to pursue the pipe dream of a British *Zollverein*, or complete free trade within the Empire and protection against the foreigner. His friend, Sir Charles Tupper, Canadian High Commissioner in London, was one of the initiators of the Imperial Commercial League which was founded early in 1895 with the purpose of securing this hopelessly idealistic objective. After the first meeting, little was heard of its activities.

Meanwhile the United Empire Trade League, with Lowther as its chief spokesman, had embarked on a campaign to educate public opinion in the practical benefits of protection and Empire preference. Conditions were not entirely propitious. At the annual meeting of the Cobden Club, Lord Farrer told his audience that the general situation was 'more satisfactory than could have been expected a short time since' and that 'the whole position is in fact very favourable'. He was referring to the improvement in the trade figures which suggested that Britain was gradually reasserting herself in the world markets. In 1894 the total value of exports amounted to only £216,006,000 (almost the same figure as in 1879) but the following year there was a significant increase which was repeated in 1896.

On the debit side, certain industries continued to suffer from severe foreign competition. The textile trade was virtually stagnant and iron production was on the decline, while farmers and estate owners faced even worse difficulties. Wheat prices which averaged over 50s a quarter between 1870 and 1875, fell to rock bottom in

1894 when the return was 22*s* 10*d*. There was a small rise in 1895 and business improved for the next three years but even in 1898 the average price was only 34*s* a quarter. By contrast, the industrial and commercial expansion in Germany and the United States showed that Britain was in serious danger of losing many of her overseas markets.

The fair traders knew that the Prime Minister was sympathetic. Salisbury was worried about the effect of foreign tariffs and had already warned the electorate: 'If you intend, in this conflict of commercial treaties, to hold your own, you must be prepared, if need be, to inflict upon the nations which injure you the penalty which is in your hands—that of refusing them access to your markets.'

The League's first move was to send a deputation to the Prime Minister in the hope of winning his patronage. Salisbury was non-committal and bearing in mind the prevailing opinion in the cabinet he had little choice.

Lowther was not discouraged and in September 1895 he presided over a Fair Trade Conference in London. The manifesto which was provisionally adopted held out the promise of better employment of the people, the restoration of agriculture and the federation of the Empire. The means was to be the promotion of Empire trade by mutual preference.

Lowther traipsed round the country addressing meetings of farmers and calling for a sliding scale of protective duties as the only policy to save agriculture. He barely mentioned the question of preference and Empire unity and, adapting his arguments to suit his audiences, who were more concerned with their own problems than with the future of the colonies, he extolled the virtues of protection for its own sake.

During the first weeks of 1896 Chamberlain had little opportunity to reflect upon the activity of the protectionists or to concentrate his mind upon the problems of Empire unity. He was entangled in the politics of South Africa and the ambitions of another imperialist. Cecil Rhodes became Prime Minister of Cape Colony in 1890. For ten years he had successfully pursued a policy of expansion, establishing Britain as the dominant power in South Africa and hemming in the Dutch-inhabited territory, the Transvaal. His ambition was to unite British and Dutch into a single state covering the southern part of the Continent. The Boers were chiefly concerned with maintaining their own civilisation, an aspiration which was made all but impossible by the flood of immigrants—mainly British—who flocked into the country to make their fortunes in the goldfields. Paul Kruger, President of the Transvaal, refused to compromise and turned down the demands of the immigrants for civic rights, and Rhodes, watching impatiently from the sidelines, was eventually persuaded to give his support to plans for a revolution which was to be backed by a force sent in from Rhodesia. The scheme went wrong. The revolt did not take place and Dr Jameson, the leader of the raising party, was ignominiously forced to surrender. It was the first scene of a tragedy which was to involve Britain in four years of colonial warfare.

And it was a setback for Chamberlain. He was immediately accused of complicity in the affair even though he promptly repudiated the Raid and the Raiders and sent a cable to Kruger offering his cooperation. A protracted and muddled inquiry failed to clear his name entirely, which was not unreasonable, for he certainly knew of a plan to send a force of troops into the Transvaal *after* a rising of the Uitlanders had taken place in Johannesburg (**54**).

The Raid was a setback for another reason. Chamberlain had expressed a strong sympathy with the movement towards union in South Africa and in Australia, where the colonies were preparing to merge their identities into a single state. His ideas on Empire unity were still at a level where, too often, pious hopes were offered in place of rational arguments. He saw the trend towards federation *within* the Empire as part of a sequence leading to federation *of* the Empire—a very optimistic conclusion—and although he showed awareness of the growing sense of independence among the colonies he overestimated his own power and that of his sympathisers to determine future developments. He should have reminded himself that Rhodes, the greatest imperialist, was also a firm believer in home rule (he supported Parnell to the tune of £10,000) and that a South Africa under his sway was unlikely to submit to direction from London.

On the other hand he recognised that the process of securing a united Empire would take many years of patient effort and he was convinced that a progressive policy must advance, as top priority, proposals for closer commercial relations between the mother country and the colonies. To this extent he was on the side of realism. But he overplayed his hand, partly because he was too inclined to take at face value the protestations of loyalty which colonial politicians frequently included in their public speeches, but chiefly because he underestimated the political and economic strength of the colonial protectionists.

During the early months of 1896 Chamberlain embarked on his campaign for Empire free trade. The timing was deliberate. Continental reaction to the Jameson Raid had revived the jingo spirit in Britain. The Kaiser's congratulatory telegram and the presentation to Kruger by France of a ceremonial sword adorned with a Boer throttling the imperial lion made Jameson a popular hero and for a time earned public abuse for the Colonial Secretary who had disowned him. Chamberlain needed to revarnish his imperial image and, in matters of Empire, public opinion was in the mood to respond to a positive lead. He was encouraged by manufacturers who were increasingly worried by the effects of German competition on British trade. Chamberlain helped to show that their fears were justified by setting up in London an impressive exhibition of foreign competitive goods recently imported by the colonies. On 25 March he spoke at a dinner of the Canada Club. Referring to the recent South Africa crises he quoted an extract from an address by a member of the Canadian Parliament (Alexander MacNeil):

> The British people are one people, animated by one spirit, and determined to stand together as one man in defence of their common rights and in the maintenance of their common interests. We desire peace before all. We regard war with horror; but we are prepared to accept it with all its consequences, come from what quarter it may, if it be necessary to do so in order to defend the honour and integrity of our own Empire.

'Our own Empire'; this was the touch which attracted Chamberlain to this fragment of emotional oratory. The problem was to transform the sentiment into reality, to create one Empire with common interests and obligations. In his speech he resurrected the idea of following the pattern of German unification and embarking on a British *Zollverein* or free trade within the Empire. It was, he said, 'a proper subject for discussion' which 'might probably lead to a satisfactory arrangement'.

He returned to the same theme when he addressed the delegates of the Congress of the Chambers of Commerce of the Empire in June 1896. Empire federation depended in the first instance upon the willingness of the members to join a customs union. Cooperation on other matters, including defence, would automatically follow.

He made clear that he regarded a *Zollverein* as a compromise solution. The colonies could maintain a protective policy against foreign imports but concede free entry to imports from the mother country and, in return, Britain would impose duties on foreign goods but continue to allow Empire products to compete on equal terms. He bluntly rejected schemes for mutual preference:

> The foreign trade of this country is so large, and the foreign trade of the colonies is comparatively so small, that a small preference given to us upon that foreign trade by the colonies would make so trifling a difference . . . that I do not believe the working classes of this country would consent to make a revolutionary change for what they would think to be an infinitesimal gain.

Reaction at home among Government supporters was favourable, but unhelpful. *The Times* brought out a patronising leader which proclaimed the benefits which would accrue to the colonies if Britain added a few articles to the dutiable list (food was not included). The Duke of Devonshire, a lifelong free-trader and leading Liberal Unionist, voiced vague approval and suggested that another conference should be held to discuss the proposals.

The protectionists expressed support for his ideals, but the Colonial Secretary, not wishing to antagonise the Tory free-traders and having little regard for protection simply as a palliative for economic ills, ignored their contribution to the debate. Vincent wrote to the Colonial Secretary enclosing with his letter a précis of the Canada Club speech which he intended to circulate as a League pamphlet. Chamberlain was cautious. He considered the abridged version to be misleading and suggested that Vincent should either print the entire speech or nothing (**3**).

The attitude of the Liberal opposition was summed up by Asquith, who concluded 'that the loose and informal connection which at present exists between the mother country and the colonies might perhaps in the long run be found to be the best and surest safeguard for the permanence of our Imperial unity'. The President of the Cobden Club, ever vigilant, described the *Zollverein* plan as a 'step backwards'. Chamberlain could not reasonably expect a national acclamation, although he was probably disappointed that his theme was not taken up by other members of the Government. The really chastening experience was the response from the colonies.

The Congress of the Chambers of Commerce of the Empire, which provided the occasion for the second of Chamberlain's *Zollverein* speeches, began well with a resolution advocating 'an arrangement, as nearly as possible of the nature of a *Zollverein*, based upon principles of the freest exchange, of commodities within the Empire'. But an amendment recommending a customs arrangement on the basis of preferential treatment was quickly proposed. In the end, the only resolution which the delegates were willing to support unanimously was one approving closer commercial relations between the various parts of the Empire and suggesting that an Imperial Conference be summoned to consider a plan if the colonies requested that the matter should be discussed.

The Australian delegates who supported imperial preference were vindicated a few days later when the Premier of Victoria completely discounted the possibility of a *Zollverein* on the grounds that local industries founded under a system of protection would not stand the strain of open competition with British imports. In July the Premier of New South Wales, the only free-trade colony in Australia, in a speech praising Britain's wise and generous trade policy, rubbed in the salt by proclaiming that 'if Britain's power must pass away, it is better to let it die a natural death than endeavour to prolong her decay by closing her wide Imperial gates'.

The only encouragement for Chamberlain was the decisive victory in the Canadian election of Laurier and the Liberal Party. Laurier was known to favour lower tariffs and it could be hoped that his attitude towards an Empire *Zollverein* would be more favourable than that of his predecessors. Before long Laurier admitted that the best that could be achieved was a lowering of tariffs on British goods while maintaining high protection against the foreigner. However, he proposed a concession of $12\frac{1}{2}$ per cent, which was soon afterwards increased to 25 per cent, in favour of British goods entering the Canadian market. It was not entirely an act of self-sacrifice. The most serious competition which British exporters faced in Canada was from the Canadian manufacturers and they remained highly protected. Textiles, for example, accounted for more than half the total of Canadian imports from Great Britain, but home production was increasing and already her output exceeded the quantity of textiles imported from the mother country. Even so the duty on printed cottons was raised from 30 per cent to 35 per cent before preference was granted (**53**).

In November 1896, in an address to the Birmingham Chamber of Commerce dealing with Britain's trade prospects, Chamberlain included no reference to the Empire *Zollverein* plan. More surprisingly, he praised Britain's open-door policy in relation to the colonies by which foreigners were given the same opportunities as home manufacturers to establish export markets in British possessions. The Cobden Club congratulated Chamberlain on his conversion. The imperial *Zollverein* was still-born, but it was not yet buried. It came up for discussion for the last time when the Premiers met in London for the 1897 Colonial Conference. After the debates Chamberlain formally admitted that the idea had, once for all, been rejected (**30**).

Canada's lead on preference was received by the Conference with greater enthusiasm and the colonies expressed a willingness to offer similar concessions. Chamberlain was only too pleased to encourage them, and later in the year the British Government responded by renouncing their trade treaties with Belgium and Germany which precluded the colonies from giving preferential treatment which did not extend to the continental signatories. The treaties had been a sore point with the colonies for some time and a demand for their renunciation was recorded at the Ottawa conference, a request which the Liberal Government had turned down on the grounds that our exports to Belgium and Germany exceeded the total of our exports to the self-governing colonies.

The United Empire Trade League triumphantly reminded the public that it had been campaigning for the termination of the treaties since 1891 and little over a year since had asked the Foreign Secretary to abrogate those clauses of the treaties which 'so improperly, unjustly and unfairly limit the development of trade within Her Majesty's Empire'.

Chamberlain had learned his lesson and, either from a sense of failure or disappointment or because of a necessary preoccupation with other matters, he temporarily abandoned his crusade for Empire federation. For the next few years, he kept his silence.

5 Conservatives and Empire

If Chamberlain was discouraged, others within the Conservative party were prepared to carry on the campaign for a trade agreement with the colonies. The protectionists were strongly represented at the Conservative Conference which was held at Rochdale in November 1896, and the debates were almost entirely concerned with trade or matters connected with trade. For those who wanted protection as a means to Empire unity and for those who wanted Empire unity as a means to protection, the Conference endorsed its previous resolutions on the subject of commercial federation and approved a resolution which called upon the Government to raise indirect taxation by imposing duties on foreign imports which competed with home manufacturers.

In the new year a comparative study of industry and commerce at home and abroad was published as a Parliamentary Paper. It was the joint effort of Sir Courtenay Boyle, Permanent Secretary of the Board of Trade and his colleague Sir Robert Giffen, who was Head of the Statistics Department. Their view of the general trade situation was cautiously optimistic. Relative increases in population had transformed the United States of America and Germany into formidable competitors, but Britain still held the lead. Even more encouraging, 'the greater proportion of the trade in non-European countries, and in British possessions everywhere is carried on with the United Kingdom. Germany runs us close in some European countries, especially in Russia and Northern Europe, but with that exception our preponderance is manifest.' The Report had a sting in its tail: the warning that, while trade was not yet seriously affected, competition would intensify. The authors did not set out to advise on this particular problem, but it was clear that exporters had a busy time ahead.

Tariffs were in the news again in March when the Prime Minister, prompted by the introduction of the new and higher Dingley tariff in the United States, revived the threat of retaliation. Speaking to the annual Conference of the Association of Chambers of Commerce, Salisbury told the delegates that Britain was entering on a period of great commercial struggle and her inability to retaliate against foreign tariffs might put her at a serious disadvantage in the fight for export markets. 'You might as well send a party to take a fortress without guns,' he said, and added, 'I am not pretending that retaliation ought to be often practised. Like war, it is a very dangerous weapon . . .'

His nephew was even more cautious. Speaking some weeks earlier in Sheffield, with Vincent in attendance, Arthur Balfour, then leader of the House of Commons, referred to that 'infinite and never-ending controversy' and satisfied himself by providing a thought for both sides. Few economists of any nation, he reminded his audience, supported protection, yet only two nations, Britain and Turkey, remained loyal to the principles of free trade.

Vincent pinned his faith on the power of the politicians to defeat the teachings of the economists. The chief problem was to find a means of converting the politicians. If Salisbury and Balfour had their doubts, the other members of the Cabinet showed no inclination to question the efficacy of free trade. Vincent kept up the pressure by using every opportunity to attack the foreigner. A somewhat petty campaign to amend the Merchandise Marks Acts was overwhelmingly defeated. The original Bill provided for foreign goods to be marked with a stamp showing their place of origin, a rule, it was argued, which served merely to advertise our competitors. Products at one time passing into the world markets through the British *entrepôt* were now purchased by direct dealing between the maker and the consumer. Paradoxically, it was also submitted that foreign manufacturers deliberately evaded the Act. Packages were marked but not the articles they contained, or the stamp was placed where it was practically invisible. One writer reported that a German firm which exported sewing machines conspicuously labelled 'Singers' and 'North-British Sewing Machines', fixed a small 'Made in Germany' label under the treadle (**65**). Vincent's Bill sought to provide a remedy for both problems. If the House of Commons had been in a receptive mood, foreign manufacturers would have found themselves bound by law to mark all their goods, clearly and indelibly with the words 'Foreign Made'.

A few weeks later Vincent at last succeeded in pushing through a protectionist Bill. For some time he had been urging the Government to take measures to ban the importation of foreign prison-made goods. The last Liberal administration had set up an investigatory committee which reported, after the Conservatives had returned to power, that the situation was not serious enough to warrant legislation. Vincent stuck to his guns and gained some unexpected support from Chamberlain and from Ritchie, President of the Board of Trade and a strong free-trader. Members who were disinclined to allow British convicts to perform constructive work found something distasteful in the revelation that foreign criminals were allowed to compete for work on equal terms with honest workmen.

The Government sponsored an appropriate Bill which passed its second reading in the House of Commons in May 1897. It was later described by Lord Farrer as 'one of the worst bits of truckling to the worst of trade union prejudices which we have ever experienced', but Chamberlain, strongly supported by Vincent, claimed that prison goods 'competed unfairly with British industry, especially in the brush and mat trades'. Whether the competition was serious or not, the Act was certainly effective. Nine months later as a result of a question in the House, the President of the Board of Trade advanced the information that the Commissioners of Customs had only once had occasion to exercise their powers. The axe had fallen on an importer who was bringing 108 bundles of Belgian mats into the country. Their total value was estimated to be £147 4s.

A far more serious situation—the distress of the West Indian sugar planters—offered an opportunity to campaign for a more effective measure of protection. The depressed state of that industry was chiefly attributed to competition from the Continent, where beet sugar production was artificially stimulated by the payment of bounties. A Royal Commission was appointed and its report was submitted early in 1898. The recommendations really amounted to a proposal to offer financial assistance to the West Indies but the Chairman, General Sir Henry Norman, accepted the opinion of witnesses who had firsthand knowledge of the industry and declared himself in favour of imposing retaliatory tariffs.

Chamberlain was immediately attracted to the idea. He wrote to Hicks-Beach, Chancellor of the Exchequer: 'I look upon a countervailing duty not as a remedy, but rather as a weapon to use in negotiations, and as an indication to the Colonies concerned that the mother country is not wholly indifferent to their interests.' Determined action would prove to Canada, and to the other colonies who might soon adopt their tariffs in favour of British exports, that the mother country was also prepared to make sacrifices for the benefit of imperial trade. But the Chancellor of the Exchequer refused to believe that a countervailing duty would force the continental sugar producers to relinquish their bounties. In any case he did not see why, for the sake of colonial sentiment, the British consumer should assume the burden of paying a higher price for his sugar. 'I must say frankly,' he told Chamberlain, 'that I do not like framing our fiscal system, not for our own benefit, but for the benefit of those who do not bear our taxation' (**4**).

The Cabinet agreed with Hicks-Beach and the idea was quietly dropped. Instead it was decided to try to settle the bounty question by negotiation. As a temporary expedient the Government opted for the majority recommendation of the Royal Commission and offered financial aid to help the West Indies over their crisis. It was left to John Morley to ask the Government if monetary grants were anything else but a bounty 'wrapped in paper of a different colour and bearing a different label'. He might also have asked if there was very much difference between supplying direct assistance to a producer and protecting a manufacturer. As Salisbury had prophesied, circumstances were compelling the Government to adopt a less rigid approach in matters of fiscal policy.

By the closing years of the century a strong section of the Tory rank and file was firmly committed to closer trade relations with the Empire and to protective policies. Opinion was influenced by the tendency among foreign competitors to drive inroads into hitherto exclusively British markets in the colonies, but taken by itself this not-so-new commercial development was insufficient to attract wide support for a major departure from the principles of free trade. A strong case was advanced by those who argued that international trade would present less of a problem if the manufacturers shook themselves out of their malaise and adapted their selling techniques to suit modern requirements [**doc. 7**].

Apart from trade, international power politics played a part in persuading many Conservatives that some means had to be found to bring the various parts of the Empire into closer cooperation. Disputes with France over territorial claims in Africa and fear of Russian expansionist ambitions in China emphasised the basic weakness of the Government's foreign policy. Britain did not have a single ally of any consequence. Chamberlain took a lead in trying to improve the situation by working for an understanding with, first, Germany and then America but his efforts were abortive. In these circumstances it is hardly surprising that the Imperialist Party should look to the Empire as a balance of the Triple Alliance (Germany, Austria and Italy) and the Franco-Russian Alliance.

The preoccupation with Empire reached its climax in the final year of the nineteenth century. The situation in South Africa had been steadily deteriorating since Jameson's humiliating failure and negotiations for better terms for the 'Uitlanders' (the unenfranchised residents in the Transvaal) had become more difficult. In 1897 Sir Alfred Milner was sent out as High Commissioner. His chief aim was to persuade Kruger to agree to five years' residence as the minimum qualification for the vote, but the old President would not go below seven years, unless Britain agreed to withdraw all claims to suzerainty based on the 1881 and 1884 Conventions, which allowed the Transvaal internal self-government. Neither side would give way. During the summer of 1899 British troops were drafted into South Africa. In October Kruger issued an ultimatum demanding the withdrawal of the military from the frontier. On the day on which the notice expired Boer troops crossed the frontier at three points, invading Natal and besieging Mafeking and Kimberly on the western boundary.

While the war continued the Colonial Secretary remained the major personality in the Government and in terms of electoral popularity overshadowed all his contemporaries. It was, after all, 'Joe's War' (**43**). The ageing Salisbury and his Cabinet were content to leave Chamberlain to manage the entire affair and he made the best of it. (In the 1900 election the Conservatives were returned with a slightly increased majority.)

Chamberlain was convinced that the war had brought the Empire closer together. The colonies had expressed support for the mother country and had provided military aid, a fact which was not lost on the British public. Chamberlain knew very well that if a move towards Empire unity was to be made at all, opinion at home and in the colonies would have to be favourably disposed to making sacrifices for the common end. The war seemed to provide an ideal opportunity and he was aware that for the first time in his career he possessed the power to exert a major influence on international policy. The question was *how* to preserve that sense of imperial unity and to transform it into a tangible and binding relationship.

For those with protectionist leanings imperial trade preference offered the last vestige of a chance of achieving the ideal. Empire patriotism, sharpened by foreign hostility, persuaded others to think along similar lines. But it needed more than Empire patriotism to persuade Chamberlain that preference was within the scope of practical politics. Another factor, stronger than the fear of foreign competition, stronger even than Empire patriotism, played its part in converting Chamberlain and many ordinary MPs who shared his initial scepticism. In the last years of the century Treasury officials and ministers concerned with finance were anxiously anticipating future demands on the slender resources of the Exchequer. Expenditure on the armed forces and on education was expected to grow automatically, the farmers were pressing for assistance, teachers were demanding pensions and the poorer sections of the community were looking forward to some sort of provision for their old age. A Treasury memorandum warned the Government that 'the question of Imperial finance may very possibly before long become a serious problem' (**4**).

Sir Michael Hicks-Beach was Chancellor of the Exchequer. Soon after taking office he convinced himself that the country was unable to bear much in the way of additional taxation and he set his heart on economies and lower government expenditure. He survived his first four budgets without resorting to tax increases, but with an annual surplus of revenue he was forced to give way to demands for fresh commitments, notably in the naval estimates. Then further demands in the military and colonial sectors raised fears of an impending deficit and in 1899 he was desperately searching for a means of restraining the financial excesses of his colleagues.

Eventually he was persuaded to call upon the taxpayer to help him foot the bill. According to Treasury advice, there was not much room for manoeuvre. Income tax stood at eightpence in the pound and was, apparently, 'already too high for times of peace'. Inevitably the Chancellor's attention was concentrated upon the narrow range of indirect taxes. In his Budget speech he announced an increase in the wine duty. On the face of it, it was not a decision likely to raise very much excitement. A small section of the electorate was affected, the tax did not offend the broad principles of free trade since there was no home wine industry to protect, and the

Chancellor could argue that he had advanced some way towards broadening the basis of taxation (a long cherished aim of the Government and its supporters). But there was one difficulty Hicks-Beach had overlooked. He was suddenly involved in an embarrassing argument with the spokesman for Empire preference.

Vincent and Lowther initiated a campaign on behalf of the Australian and Cape wine producers. A conference at the offices of the United Empire Trade League, at which Australian representatives were present, decided to send a deputation to the Prime Minister to request that the increased wine tax should not apply to the Empire. Vincent announced that he intended to move an appropriate amendment to the Finance Bill.

The Board of Trade estimated that the Exchequer would stand to lose a mere twenty thousand pounds in a full year. International goodwill was seldom purchasable at such a price. But the proposal encountered heavy criticism from the departmental advisers on the grounds that Empire preference 'would entail a reversal of the trade policy so long and persistently adopted by this country' (4). Vincent's amendment was defeated but he guessed there would be other opportunities to continue the argument. In time of crisis the Treasury would inevitably resort to taxes on trade as the only means of limiting the load on the narrow shoulders of the income tax payer.

The crisis came. British ministers at war were far more demanding than British ministers at peace. Hicks-Beach had no choice but to find the necessary capital. In 1900 the income tax was raised from eightpence to one shilling. Taxes on tea, beer and spirits and the duty on tobacco and cigars were all increased. Lowther appealed for preference for the tea-producing colonies. The Chancellor refused. In 1901 income tax was again raised this time to one shilling and twopence. Coal was subjected to an export duty of one shilling a ton and the import duties on sugar were restored. Vincent asked the Chancellor if he intended to except West Indian sugar. He received a short, firm reply: 'No, Sir.'

The Government was in a peculiar difficulty which many commentators failed to recognise. The *Spectator* comfortably observed that Hicks-Beach had avoided giving a protective inclination to his new taxes and had spurned the advances of those 'who would like to see what they describe as a system of free trade within the Empire, but of protection from without'. But the journal ignored the fact that some of the duties were eminently suitable vehicles for imperial preference simply because their purpose was not to protect home industries. How could the Government refuse the modest claims of the colonial exporters? On the other hand if preference was established it would imply a fundamental change in British fiscal policy. And who was to say where that would end?

The problem was capable of solving itself if the duties were only temporary measures introduced to meet the requirements of a short war time emergency. In this case the Chancellor could sensibly oppose going through the rigmarole of introducing imperial concessions which might operate for less than a year. But Hicks-Beach was not convinced that the duties could be lifted even if the war ended quickly. His 1901 Budget speech revealed that the deficit of over £55 million could not be entirely blamed on the war. There had been an 'alarming' growth in ordinary expenditure, despite his ruthless application of the principles of economy. In 1902 income tax was raised by just one penny. Hick-Beach had said too much about 'broadening the basis of taxation' to risk a larger increase. He cast around for ideas for spreading the burden.

One possible innovation had been lengthily discussed. In 1895 a Treasury official wrote: 'It is probable that, were it necessary to have recourse to the reimposition of a former indirect tax, the duty which would be singled out off-hand by most people as the most obvious one to be re-enacted would be "the shilling duty" [on corn].' But 'it is tolerably certain that any proposal to subject wheat to the smallest import duty would revive the old controversy about the "big loaf" and the "little loaf". It would be regarded as a retrograde step, and as the first move in the direction of protection' (4).

Hicks-Beach calculated if he kept the duty down to one shilling and disclaimed any intention of protecting the farmer he could escape criticism.

In his Budget speech in April 1902 the Chancellor announced his decision. The Empire preference noose which the Government had voluntarily strung round its own neck was jerked tight.

Immediately, the Opposition interpreted the corn duty as a major victory for the protectionists. Tariffs on wine, tea and sugar were dwarfed by comparison with this latest violation of the rules of free trade. The poor, said the Liberals, were being asked to add to their burdens by assuming the cost of defending the agricultural industry from the effects of foreign competition. The Government plaintively asserted that the duty had been imposed for revenue purposes only and, in any case, was too small either to influence the price of bread or to result in any material benefit for the farmers.

Their case might have appeared stronger had the protectionist back benchers exercised some restraint. But Vincent and his friends were in no mood to consider the best interests of the Administration. They regarded the corn duty as their breakthrough and vied with each other to heap compliments on the embarrassed Chancellor. Henry Chaplin, having relinquished his ministerial post, joined them in enthusiastically supporting an innovation which he had long advocated (**47**). Winston Churchill noted their jubilation and speculated on what would happen if the fair trade issue was openly raised by some person of authority and eminence in the country. He did not have to wait long for an answer.

On 13 May Campbell-Bannerman led an attack on the Government's financial policy which helped to establish his leadership and revived the spirits of his followers. During his speech he referred to a statement by the Canadian Prime Minister which suggested that he regarded the corn duty as a means of introducing reciprocal trade preferences. Balfour vainly denied that the Government had deliberately brought in the shilling duty to facilitate a closer commercial relationship with the colonies. Soon the colonial premiers were to meet in London for their coronation year conference. It was inconceivable that matters of trade should be excluded from the agenda: inconceivable too that pressure would not be exerted on Britain to grant concessions to the wheat producers of the Empire. Inevitably, the next logical step was to negotiate a mutually acceptable preferential policy. If the Government had not purposely engineered this sequence of events they stood condemned for something far worse: gross incompetence or a blatant disregard for colonial opinion.

Members of both sides of the House of Commons suspected a plot. They were wrong. The average minister was a convinced free-trader. He was not well informed on economic questions but his faith was strong. The corn duty was accepted because Hicks-Beach gave an assurance that his aim was not to protect the home market. Unfortunately they quite forgot the imperial factor. When the storm broke they were taken by surprise and bungled their excuses. Working hard from their defensive position, the party leaders lavished praise on the Chancellor and his tax. They fastened themselves to what was, apparently, an indispensable component of the

modern fiscal system. The colonial premiers were not alone in
believing that the corn duty would remain so long as the Tories
held power. Chamberlain was one minister who was fully conscious
of the implications. For the first time in his political career he
visualised imperial preference in terms of practical politics.

Hicks-Beach was given the chance to reply to his critics when he
spoke during the debate on the Finance Bill. He denied that the
Government intended deliberately to set up duties against foreign
nations in order to give an advantage to the colonies. At the same
time he was sympathetic to any plan which might lead to free trade
within the Empire and to the establishment of an imperial *Zollverein* (**35**). The Opposition was quick to spot the ambiguity in his
line of reasoning. If the Cabinet were now prepared to lend their
support to an imperial *Zollverein* might not a concession on the corn
duty be a logical first step towards the ideal? Nothing could have
been further from the Chancellor's mind but his clumsy attempt to
clarify the Government's motive without appearing indifferent to the
imperial trade connection was regarded by many of his opponents
as a clever technique to avoid a direct answer.

In mid-June interest shifted to the arrival in Britain of the colonial
prime ministers. Seddon, the New Zealand Premier, was welcomed
at Southampton on the 15th. Referring to the Conference he told a
Reuter's representative that 'the most important question by far is
that of the trade and tariff relations of the Empire', and a few days
later he elaborated on this statement by devoting a major portion
of a speech to the advocation of imperial preference. The Empire
could be self-sufficient he argued but if Britain did not 'wake up',
much of her imperial trade would be lost to the foreign competitor.

Barton, the Australian Prime Minister, was much more cautious.
When he and Seddon spoke at the 'luncheon of welcome' organised
by the United Empire Trade League they provided an interesting
contrast. Seddon let fly a volley of ideas, suggestions and criticisms.
He exhibited a real sympathy for the purposes of the League. Barton
was reserved and limited his comments on the trade question to a
broad observation that commerce between the mother country and
the colonies was steadily advancing. Two years later the Governor
General of Australia, Lord Northcote, described him as a 'jumping
cat' and added: 'He is a Free Trader, but, though these are his
principles, "if you don't like them gentlemen they can be altered",
so long as he makes the alteration' (**1**).

Laurier was also cautious, but for different reasons. Of all the countries in the Empire the corn tax chiefly affected Canada. Economically, a concession to the prairie farmers was worth having and Laurier also wanted to satisfy his critics that Britain was prepared to make some return for the Canadian preference on British products. Yet he knew that he would need all his political skill to overcome the free trade prejudices of the Imperial Government.

The Colonial Conference was the first major event of Balfour's premiership (Salisbury retired in July), but the direction of the negotiations was entirely the responsibility of Chamberlain, who entered upon the task with his usual enthusiasm. His opening speech outlined the immediate priorities and linked them to an appeal for a closer Imperial connection. 'I may be considered, perhaps, to be a dreamer,' he told the delegates, '. . . but I do not hesitate to say that, in my opinion the political federation of the Empire is within the limits of possibility.'

It was an inspiring thought, but Chamberlain was not resurrecting the high-flown idealism of the 1880s and '90s. He had learned the difference between long-term possibilities and short-run practicalities and he suggested merely that the Conference might set off on the right lines if it instituted an Imperial Council which could advise the Government on Empire matters. But this mild proposal was greeted without enthusiasm and the colonial delegates ran true to form by quietly forestalling a move which might affect their power of independent decision.

On the question of imperial commerce Chamberlain knew that his government colleagues were unwilling to formulate a realistic policy. He had no choice but to leave the initiative with the colonies.

They were unanimous in regarding Empire free trade as entirely impracticable, but they endorsed the principle of preferential trade and agreed to recommend the adoption of varying rates of preference on British goods entering their markets. At the same time they took good care to allow themselves the choice of either lowering duties in favour of the United Kingdom or (more likely) instituting preference by raising or imposing duties on foreign goods and thereby leaving their own manufacturers heavily protected. The mother country was not required to abandon her traditional trade policy but at the insistence of Laurier she was bluntly asked to reciprocate by granting an 'exemption from or reduction of duties *now or hereafter imposed*' (5).

It was now clear that the colonies were not prepared to make further trade concessions until Britain could guarantee to them a larger share of the home market. In particular Laurier expected preferential treatment for the Canadian corn producers. The colonies also hinted that unless Britain modified her fiscal policy to suit the requirements of the dominions, she could not expect them to assume their share of the responsibility for imperial defence and foreign policy. Trade privileges were the only return Britain could make for assistance which she badly needed.

While the colonial delegates were busy with their discussions the public temporarily lost interest in the future of the corn duty and turned its attention to other matters. The war in South Africa dragged to a close and the nation celebrated the Peace of Pretoria. At the same time preparations were under way for a June Coronation which was suddenly postponed when it was learned that the King was suffering from an attack of appendicitis. A successful operation for what was then a serious illness, followed by the ceremonies and pageantry of a new reign, engendered a mood of national confidence and well being. The Tories detected the dawning of a 'new epoch'.

In this atmosphere it was unthinkable that the Colonial Conference should be represented as anything but a gathering of harmonious voices and an official communiqué blandly reported that the trade and defence negotiations had been 'successful from the Imperial point of view'. The publication of the resolutions was delayed until November. Details of the discussions remained secret. Even when the country returned to normal the tariff question remained in the political backwater. The Government was preoccupied with the repercussions of the Education Act, which provided aid to Church schools and was interpreted by the Nonconformists as a means of providing the Church of England with a disguised subsidy. For the first time in seven years the Liberal Party acted as a united and determined Opposition and enthusiastically promoted the Nonconformist revolt (**63**). Chamberlain, himself a Nonconformist and a strong believer in the principle of free secular education, worked hard to avoid a split in the ranks of the Liberal Unionists. For the sake of the party which was, at least, pledged to preserve Ireland and South Africa as imperial possessions, he surrendered his convictions and supported the Education Act.

Perhaps Chamberlain calculated that he deserved some return for his loyalty. Perhaps he was simply 'an old man in a hurry'. Whatever

49

his motive, in October he chose to remind his colleagues of the resolutions agreed by the Colonial Conference and to inform them that in his opinion the corn duty should be used for the purpose of negotiating a scheme of mutual preference with Canada. No one can give a precise account of the discussions of that Cabinet meeting. Certainly Chamberlain went away with the impression that, in principle, the Cabinet had accepted his proposal and his supporters later accused the Government of fomenting a crisis in the party by retracting their decision (**30**).

On the very day of the meeting Balfour, who was inclined to support Chamberlain on this issue, informed the King that he 'only permitted [the] discussion on the distinct understanding that no premature decision was to be taken upon it' (**25, 67**) but the following August in a letter to the Duke of Devonshire he referred to the Chancellor's '*unexpected* refusal to embody [the concession to colonial corn producers] in his Budget', adding, 'and this after he [Chamberlain] had just reason to suppose that in November the Cabinet as a whole were in its favour' (**1**).

Was the Chancellor himself? Hicks-Beach, the instigator of the corn duty, had resigned with Salisbury. For some years past he had felt the strain of his work but he finally made up his mind to leave when he realised that he could not rely on Balfour to back his demands for stricter controls on Government spending. According to Lord George Hamilton, a colleague who shared his distaste for the 'increasing burden of expenditure', he made the mistake of pitching his demands too high by attempting to 'get guarantees from Balfour as regards our future fiscal and financial policy, which it was quite impossible for any Prime Minister to give' (**2**).

His successor was Charles Ritchie, a strong free-trader, whose concept of the functions of the national economy was closely in line with the opinion of the ex-Chancellor. His immediate reaction to a preferential corn duty was unfavourable, but Chamberlain had caught him by surprise and he took shelter behind the argument that it was premature to attempt to settle the Budget for the ensuing year, eight months in advance. The other free-traders in the Cabinet followed his line. They needed time to construct a case against corn preference which did not require them to admit either that the imperial connection was of no consequence or that the original shilling duty was protective in character.

Thus Chamberlain and Balfour left the Cabinet meeting with the impression that their colleagues had no objection in principle to preferential treatment for colonial what importers. The free trade group, which included Ritchie, the Duke of Devonshire (Lord President), Lord George Hamilton (Secretary of State for India) and Lord Balfour of Burleigh (Secretary of State for Scotland), were equally convinced that the entire question remained wide open **(33)**.

Towards the end of November, Chamberlain departed on his visit to South Africa. Birmingham gave him a great send-off. A lavish banquet was prepared and at the end of the evening 4,000 torchbearers escorted him to his home. Many politicians would have regarded a demonstration on this scale as a fitting climax to a successful career. Not so Chamberlain; for him it marked the opening stages of a new campaign.

6 Tariff Reform

There was fog and rain in Southampton on the morning of 14 March 1903, when Chamberlain returned from his triumphal tour in South Africa. But not even the weather could dampen the spirits of those who were waiting to welcome him. No sooner had he and his wife stepped down the gangplank than they were met by a deputation of his constituents, headed by his Chairman.

'They were all beaming when I expressed my surprise at seeing them', wrote Mrs Chamberlain in a letter to her mother. '. . . Their great delight was in having been the first to greet him—even before the family.'

On the last leg of the journey home there were other, more spontaneous, signs of welcome. 'What was a real surprise to us [was] to find that as we passed through the stations in the "special" . . . little crowds were gathered to see the train go by—and that in the fields groups were assembled, and from back gardens and windows flags and handkerchiefs and hats were waved to us as the train flew by' (3).

Chamberlain's popularity was by no means a safe guide to the electoral standing of the Government. The exhilaration of the war was forgotten, and Ministers were faced with a growing movement in favour of social reform at a time when their traditional supporters were calling for a return to the prewar level of Exchequer expenditure. Among a crop of by-election disasters the most significant and ominous result was that announced at Woolwich where the Labour candidate successfully attacked a Unionist stronghold and was returned with a majority of over three thousand. The irony of the situation was that the Government's single major act of social legislation—the Education Bill—was serving to strengthen the opposition in the constituencies.

Chamberlain's colleagues hoped that he would use his strong personal following to put some fighting strength back into the party. But he was not prepared to play the role expected of him. For one

thing, he was ill and very tired, but more important, he was un-
happy with the general trend of Government policy, particularly
in relation to preferential trade. During his absence, the Cabinet
had discussed the implications of a preferential corn duty. Among the
inveterate free-traders, instinctive opposition to Chamberlain and
his schemes had hardened. Ritchie worked hard to persuade
waverers to toe the free-trade line. In February he issued a Cabinet
memorandum pointing out 'with what rapidity our ordinary
expenditure has grown of late, and . . . how it has absorbed most of
the produce of the extra taxation imposed on account of the war'.

He calculated nonetheless that he had over £8 million available
for the remission of taxation. His first duty, as he saw it, was to
lower the income tax. He also reasoned it would be politic to reduce
the burden of indirect taxation on the poorer section of the community and to do this his most obvious move was to abolish the corn
duty (**2**).

Ritchie correctly assumed that the proposed corn preference
would lead to demands for further concessions. But another of his
arguments—that preference would lead to loss of revenue—was
more suspect. Apart from corn, imports on which duties were
payable included sugar (4*s* 2*d* per cwt) tea (6*d* per quarter) and
several less important commodities like wine, cocoa, coffee, currants,
raisins, spirits and tobacco. These duties could not in any sense be
regarded as protective since, unlike the corn tax, they were imposed
on commodities entirely produced abroad. Tea and sugar each
brought in an approximate revenue of £6 million; the corn tax
produced about £3 million. Assuming that the maximum preference
was offered to the colonies, the Chancellor could expect to lose
roughly £1½ million on sugar and corn and over £5 million on tea
(90 per cent of the tea imports came from India and Ceylon). Even
allowing for preferential concession on other products the total loss
was within the scope of the Exchequer surplus which Ritchie
intended giving back to the tax payers. And if, later, further duties
on foreign goods were introduced, the Exchequer could expect to
make a sizeable gain.

In the end it was Chamberlain, not Ritchie, who forced the
issue. So long as preference was firmly discounted the Chancellor
was prepared, however unwillingly, to retain the corn duty and
accompany his reduction in the income tax with a remission on tea
and sugar. But for Chamberlain it was either the corn duty and

preference or no corn duty at all. The problem was discussed by the Cabinet, with Chamberlain in attendance, during the last week in March. No agreement was reached. There was still no decision when the Cabinet met during the morning of 23 April, the day on which Ritchie had to announce his Budget proposals to the House of Commons. Chamberlain made a final attempt to gather support for imperial preference and in reply the Chancellor read a memorandum from the Chief Whip urging, on behalf of a number of Conservative MPs, the repeal of the corn duty (**37**). The majority was still inclined to favour its retention, but faced with Chamberlain's blank refusal to accept it on any but his own terms, they adopted the only possible compromise solution. The corn duty was repealed.

Chamberlain's honour was saved. At least, he did not have to report to the Canadians that the Government intended to keep the duty on corn while refusing preference to the colonial producers. In these circumstances there could have been little chance of salvaging the high ideals of imperial sentiment. Nevertheless his disappointment was intense. The introduction of the corn duty, the resolutions of the Colonial Conference, his grand tour of South Africa (which was followed by the news that the colonies in that region of the Empire were to provide for preferential treatment of British and colonial goods in those circumstances where preference was reciprocated)—these events were links in a jigsaw puzzle called Empire Unity. Like a child preoccupied with his hobby he was amazed when he discovered that his friends did not share his enthusiasm; shocked when, instead of giving him a missing piece, they trampled and destroyed his half-completed pattern.

For the time being the Government was not inclined to worry about Chamberlain's next move. By any standards Ritchie's Budget speech was an outstanding example of tactlessness and ineptitude. The announcement of the remission of the corn duty was made in such a way as to suggest that the tax had been introduced, not by his allies, but by political enemies who wanted to increase the suffering of the poor.

Ritchie's performance delighted the Opposition but embarrassed the Conservative members who, a short time ago, had stoutly defended the imposition of the corn duty. The protectionists, in particular, were furious with the Government for committing what they regarded as an act of political cowardice.

Vincent was ill and not present at the debate but Chaplin was able to take the lead in organising the agriculturalists against the Government. On 1 May he addressed a letter to the secretaries of the chief Chambers of Commerce throughout the country, calling upon them to oppose the abolition of the corn duty. A week later, Hamilton was noting the 'indication that the end of our administration is nearer than outsiders would believe' (2).

His premonition was staggeringly accurate. Chamberlain delivered his famous Tariff Reform speech in which he publicly admitted his conversion to imperial preference on 15 May before a large audience of his Birmingham constituents [**doc. 8**]. It was inevitable that he should make some statement on the subject if only to persuade the colonies that he had not betrayed their interests by meekly submitting to the decision to abolish the corn duty. It is unreasonable to assume that at this stage he was embarking on a deliberate campaign against the Government and it was more his sense of personal defeat and disillusionment which made him go well beyond the bounds of the individual initiative normally permitted to a Cabinet minister. He was probably sincere when he claimed that the excitement caused by his declared support for imperial preference came to him as a great surprise [**doc. 9**].

That the repercussions were even more serious than the Government might otherwise have expected was chiefly due to a matter of timing. At the last Cabinet meeting Balfour had reported his intention of making some guarded reference to fiscal reform in his answer to a deputation who had requested an interview in connection with the repeal of the corn duty. Chamberlain had observed that at Birmingham he would say much the same as the Prime Minister, 'only in a less definite manner'. Balfour noted somewhat petulantly, 'The famous Birmingham Speech embodied his practical endeavour to carry out this undertaking' (1).

His irritation was understandable. On the very day that Chamberlain was proclaiming the new imperialism the Prime Minister was defending the abolition of the corn duty and informing the deputation that its revival was conceivable only when the 'conscience and intellect' of the general mass of the people was disposed to accept colonial preference (25).

The difference in emphasis was at once apparent and critics detected a serious division in the Government forces. 'The machine has got out of gear', wrote Hamilton, a few hours before Chamberlain delivered his speech, 'though its creaking at present is only heard by those engaged in its management' (2). Now the creaking was louder and the sound carried beyond the Cabinet room.

Balfour was determined, above all other considerations, to maintain the unity of the Party. His obvious course, therefore, was to seek out a compromise which would reconcile Chamberlain without finally alienating the free traders. For this he needed time to bring the two sides together, and time to sort out his own ideas on the subject.

A Commons debate on preference was held on 28 May 1903, the day Parliament adjourned for the Whitsun recess. Balfour put up a spirited defence of Chamberlain and at the same time tried to impart a sense of Government unity by suggesting that the question would form the basis of a careful study. 'It is not a question that this House will have to decide this Session, or next Session, or the Session after. . . .' Eventually, however, a policy would evolve. He concluded:

I am not certain that this [Chamberlain's] scheme is practicable—but I am certain that unless this scheme proves to be practicable or unless some other scheme having the same results can be brought to fruition, and if the British Empire is to remain as it is at present, a series of isolated economic units, it is vain for us to hope that this branch . . . of the great Anglo-Saxon race is destined to have the great industrial and political future which undoubtedly lies before the United States of America.

It was a superb performance. Within a single speech he had expressed his sympathy with Chamberlain's principles, his regard for imperial solidarity and his appreciation of the deep-rooted fears of his free-trade colleagues. He might well have saved his breath. In the debate which followed Chamberlain was once again goaded into launching an animated defence of his views: a tax on food, help to agriculture, revenue for social reform, retaliation against foreign tariffs, imperial unity—a complete policy served up for immediate consumption. The free-traders were furious.

The Duke of Devonshire, Ritchie, George Wyndham, Lord Balfour of Burleigh and Lord George Hamilton sent letters to the Prime Minister, expressing their anxiety (**13**). Balfour pleaded for a calm approach to the problem. He admitted 'that if Chamberlain is to be at liberty to express his views on one side of the question, a like liberty must necessarily be extended to his colleagues to express their views on the other' (**37**). But they would have to face the fact that bickering among the leaders of the Party could result in the collapse of the Government.

Balfour was still searching for a compromise and it was clear that the free-traders were prepared to wait only if there was some guarantee of Chamberlain's good faith. At the Cabinet meeting on 9 June he was presented with an ultimatum. He was made to realise that another outburst on his part was likely to break the Government. Other considerations aside, his growing support in the country convinced him that if the Government held together there was a hopeful prospect of achieving a major breakthrough in terms of fiscal policy. He was therefore prepared to allow Balfour the chance of applying his formula. A statement was prepared which referred merely to the desirability of an inquiry into the various aspects of imperial preference.

The second reading of the Finance Bill was resumed the following day and Chaplin spoke on a motion condemning the Government for removing the corn duty. Only the Colonial Secretary was spared from his invective.

But if he expected Chamberlain to respond, he was disappointed. The Colonial Secretary sat alone at the obscurer end of the Front Bench in the shadow of the Speaker's Chair. 'With folded arms, closed eyes, countenance of strong impassivity, he sits and listens as if they were talking about someone else,' wrote one observer. No doubt he was embarrassed by the support of the old-style protectionists for whom the unity of the Empire was a secondary consideration.

It was left to Hicks-Beach to generate excitement in the debate and the Government and Opposition benches were crowded to hear the Chancellor who had originated the corn duty. He opened with a mild defence of his fiscal innovation which, he said, had performed its essential function of raising revenue without increasing the price of bread or introducing protection. What good reason could there be for the Government to abolish the duty? Hicks-Beach answered his own question. The repudiation of colonial preference was sufficient justification for the Government's decision. Despite the fact that he had contributed more than any other single politician towards raising the issues of protection and colonial preference, Hicks-Beach stood forth as the champion of free trade and ended his speech by soundly condemning the tariff reformers who sought to destroy the Unionist Party.

Now the back bench free-traders had found a leader, a respected politician who was in no way hampered by Cabinet commitments. The lines of battle were beginning to take shape.

7 Political Crisis

The Cabinet truce was reinforced by Balfour's determination to avoid parliamentary discussion on the subject of tariff reform for the remainder of the session. In theory, the breathing space would create an atmosphere in which they could carry out a calm and dispassionate reappraisal of the national economic policy. Unfortunately, Balfour was unable to extend his control beyond the immediate Government circle and his colleagues were disturbed in their deliberations by the shrill war cries of free-traders and protectionists throughout the country.

During May and the first half of June 1903, Chamberlain was riding on the crest of a tidal wave. Free-traders in the Party were stunned by the onrush of protectionist sentiment which threatened to engulf them. But in their calmer moments they noticed that the Colonial Secretary's campaign suffered one serious weakness. His sympathisers were drawn largely from the upper and middle classes—men whose chief interest centred on the profit margins of their various commercial enterprises. For them, protection was the chief object and imperial preference was a secondary consideration. Their financial and social power guaranteed them all the publicity they required, but there was no indication either now or later that the ordinary voters would allow themselves to be easily converted.

Chambers of Commerce, meeting in different parts of the country, welcomed Chamberlain's initiative, and an assortment of titled gentlemen with interests in agriculture and industry formed a Protectionist League to propagate his views. With the same purpose in mind, Lowther organised a Tariff League for Unionist MPs who favoured a 'readjustment of our fiscal system upon protectionist lines'. Before long the Tariff Reform League, Chamberlain's own creation, became the focal point of the activities of the protectionists, and a Tariff Commission was set up to enquire into the state of British trade. Most of the fifty-eight commissioners were wealthy businessmen. The colonial response to Chamberlain's proposals was largely favourable.

Apart from the efforts of Liberal Party spokesmen, the first signs of organised opposition to Chamberlain outside Parliament came from the trade unions. The link-up between social reform and tariff reform did not prove to be an outstanding attraction and the miners castigated him for his 'wanton insults to the workers and trade unionists of the country'. Chamberlain took an early opportunity to reply to his trade union critics by publishing his letter to a working man who had written to him on the subject of tariff reform and old-age pensions. He dismissed the views of the Labour leaders and held out a promise that 'a large scheme for the provision of . . . pensions to all who have been thrifty and well-conducted would be assured by a revision of our system of import duties' (**30**).

For a short time he persevered with his ambition of securing social reform without antagonising the income tax payer. But those who most needed that help were naturally averse to paying a major portion of the cost through taxes on food. There was a growing conviction, strengthened by Arthur Henderson's election as the Labour member for Barnard Castle, that welfare schemes should be financed exclusively by the wealthier classes. After June Chamberlain seldom referred to pensions and when the Cabinet truce came to an end, he adopted the line that a food tax would be more than compensated by a reduction of duties on articles such as cocoa and coffee, which were not affected by imperial preference.

On 16 June it was announced that a meeting of Unionist MPs who were in sympathy with free-trade principles would be held in the House of Commons the following week. Fifty-four MPs turned up and formed the Unionist Free Food League. The choice of name was significant for it was apparent to Chamberlain's opponents that their strongest weapon was their outright opposition to the taxation of food.

Meanwhile, Balfour was successfully preventing any discussion on the question of imperial preference and protection. He maintained that while the Enquiry was in progress a parliamentary debate was bound to be inconclusive.

The free-traders worked off their frustration by building up their propaganda organisation. The House of Lords set up a Free Trade League, and the Cobden Club opened its attack against the new protectionism. On the opposing side the Birmingham Unionist

Association formed a tariff committee to distribute leaflets which sought to justify Chamberlain's proposals.

On 21 July the Tariff Reform League held its first meeting in London. Leo Amery, who had been chief *Times* war correspondent in South Africa, was one of the leading spirits in this new non-party organisation. By mid-August, with C. Arthur Pearson, proprietor of the *Daily Express*, as its chairman, the League had set up head-quarters in Victoria Street and was working on the production and distribution of tariff reform propaganda. Chamberlain's supporters were stimulated by his public announcement that he would end the truce in the first week of October when he planned to embark upon his country-wide campaign in support of imperial preference. He already guessed that the Government enquiry into the subject was heading for failure. Expert opinion was seldom made available to ministers, who were confused by a mass of hastily compiled statistics. The responsibility largely rested with Balfour who was not eager to accept any proposal which threatened to prolong the investigation.

In late July he sent to Devonshire what he described as 'the first, and longest, instalment of my lucubration on our present economic situation', in which he gave advance notice of a Cabinet memorandum, known later as the Blue Paper, which contained proposals he hoped would satisfy the entire Government. He advocated imperial preference and retaliatory duties directed at countries which discriminated against British goods. But his policy was subject to three vital principles:

1. No retaliatory duty should be threatened, or fiscal preference offered, *with a view to protecting any industry in this country against legitimate competition*. If such duty and preference incidentally carried with it some small protection to the home producer, this would not necessarily condemn it; *but protection must not be its primary object.*

2. No such duty and no such preference should introduce any change into our fiscal system which would increase the average cost of living to the working man.

3. I do not think that, as present advised, we ought to attempt to carry out a retaliatory policy by the continental method of *starting with heavy protective duties against the world*, and then relaxing them in favour of those countries which gave us privileges . . . (**37**).

It is clear from these notes that Balfour did not intend to surrender to Chamberlain. For example, his first rule stipulated that
broadly speaking there was to be no protection against fair competition. The rule was not completely watertight since it was possible for a foreign power to set up a high tariff wall, which could not
be reduced without the threat or enforcement of retaliatory measures,
and at the same time engage in legitimate competition in the
British market by refraining from dumping or handing out subsidies to her producers. Hence the proviso that some tariffs might,
as an incidental effect, involve protection against fair competition.
But Balfour's chief object was to promote free trade and it was
therefore not part of his policy to introduce tariffs, which were not
justified on other grounds, in order to give preference to the colonies
even though preference would be allowed on tariffs imposed for
retaliatory purposes. His rule also implied that if retaliation was
successful, as he intended it should be, and foreign powers abandoned
unfair competition or reduced their tariffs on condition that Britain
made similar concession, the value of the preference on colonial
goods would decline or entirely disappear. Imperial preference was
therefore secondary to the main policy of retaliation.

While the Government was considering Balfour's statements of
aims, a Cabinet meeting was fixed for 13 August. The Prime
Minister hoped that his formula would meet with the approval of the
free-trader and protectionist ministers. He believed that the Devonshire group might reasonably accept the need for tariff retaliation
(Balfour argued that his policy would work in the interest of free
trade), while Chamberlain and his allies, realising that they were
unlikely to gain overall control of the Party, were expected to
settle for an arrangement which allowed for imperial preference
within the scope of the Government's retaliatory measures. There
was one serious drawback to the Prime Minister's plan. The free-
traders feared, above all, a tax on food. But unless duties on agricultural products were included in the list of retaliatory tariffs the
colonies, who were chiefly primary producers, could not be expected
to gain any advantage from preferential concessions. The day before
the Cabinet meeting Balfour learned that he would not succeed in
his first attempt to reach a settlement.

'I gather', said the Duke of Devonshire in a letter to the Prime
Minister, 'that we may be asked at once to assent to, or dissent from
the opinions expressed in the Memo [Blue Paper] which has been

circulated. In that case I am afraid that as at present advised I could not give any such assent, however qualified as to the practical measures which would be subsequently proposed' (**37**). Balfour spent most of the following months trying to persuade the Duke to accept his formula.

On 9 September Devonshire received the details of the plan, worked out by Balfour and Chamberlain, for the introduction of imperial preference within the scope of legitimate retaliation. Duties on meat, fruit and dairy produce were to be offset by a reduction in the taxes on tea, coffee, cocoa and sugar. It was not intended to place an import duty on corn. Even with this major concession Devonshire informed the Prime Minister that he could not accept the propositions without qualifications. His mood was downcast ('I am too old to begin a new study'), and it was obvious that he had resigned himself to the disruption of the Government. He was still the complete free-trader.

Hamilton, Ritchie, and Burleigh were of the same mind, but Balfour was beyond the point of worrying about their opinions. At one stage he believed that if his appeal for a compromise was accepted by Devonshire, they would follow his example. He was soon disillusioned, and reconciled himself to losing their political services if a hint of imperial preference appeared in the Government's policy.

On 9 September *Punch* published a cartoon which showed Balfour in cycling kit standing at a road junction. The signpost pointed to Chatsworth (Devonshire's estate) and Highbury (Chamberlain's home), which were in opposite directions. The cartoon was titled 'The Parting of the Ways' and the caption read: 'Well! Now I suppose I really must make up my mind.' Balfour was saved from making the choice, not by his own exertions, but as a result of a decision by Chamberlain.

The tariff reformers had moved some way towards a compromise. While unable to retract their demand for the taxation of food, they had lowered their sights to the extent of excepting corn and they were prepared to consider tariff rates which were far lower than those originally proposed. Unfortunately the free-traders were fighting for certain well defined principles and nothing short of an unconditional surrender was likely to satisfy them. Chamberlain was losing patience. His efforts in the Cabinet were fruitless and his self-imposed exile from the public platform left his followers without a capable leader at a time when the struggle for power in the constituencies was building up to a climax.

But there were some compensations. Balfour was sympathetic to his ideals and since the irreconcilable free-traders were likely to resign, Chamberlain could reasonably expect to remain a powerful member of a Cabinet pledged to implement fiscal reform. It is not, therefore, immediately clear why he decided at this stage to suggest to Balfour that he should resign in order to put into operation his alternative plan for a countrywide campaign to popularise imperial unity. He further proposed that while the Government pushed ahead with tariff retaliation, imperial preference should be omitted from the official policy.

One possibility is that Balfour put the idea into his head. The Prime Minister was having second thoughts on his policy. At first he had believed that duties on selected food imports might be safely included in his scheme to impose retaliatory tariffs. Now he was convinced that the taxation of food, which was necessary for imperial preference, would prove highly unpopular with the electorate. And there was also the problem of securing Devonshire's political backing to keep up the strength of the Government—a problem unlikely to be solved unless preference and Chamberlain were dropped. On the other hand there was no indication that Chamberlain's defection would be less damaging to the unity of the Party than the loss of Devonshire.

The available evidence suggests that Balfour had not seriously entertained the thought of the Colonial Secretary's withdrawal from the Government until he received his letter proposing resignation on 10 September. When Akers-Douglas, the Conservative Chief Whip, wrote to the King's private secretary to inform him that Cabinet changes were imminent, one possible and two probable resignations were mentioned; those of Burleigh, Ritchie and Hamilton. The reply from Lord Knollys (dated 13 September 1903) contained several suggestions from the King on the question of filling the vacancies. There was certainly no difference of opinion as to the candidate best suited to succeed Ritchie. 'The King', wrote Knollys ' . . . quite agrees [with the Prime Minister] that Mr Chamberlain must be Chancellor of the Exchequer, and as regards the vacancy which would then occur at the C[olonial] O[ffice] he thinks that either Lord Balfour of Burleigh, if he remains or Lord Selborne would fill it very well' (**8**).

It seems clear from the correspondence between Akers-Douglas and Knollys that Chamberlain was acting on his own initiative when he wrote to the Prime Minister. Independently, he had arrived at the same conclusion as Balfour and was now persuaded that the country was not ready to accept his policy. The opposition to the taxation of food was certainly gaining strength. On 2 September the result was declared of the by-election in Argyllshire, which had been fought chiefly on the fiscal issue. The Conservative candidate, a supporter of Chamberlain, was unable to defend the Government majority of over 600 and his free trade Liberal opponent was elected by the safe margin of 1,586. Less than a week later the verdict of the Scottish electors was reinforced by the Trade Union Congress which completed the first day of its proceedings with an overwhelming vote condemning 'the change proposed by Mr Chamberlain in our present fiscal policy as most mischievous and dangerous'.

The Colonial Secretary was faced with the alternative of either freeing himself from his Cabinet responsibilities and going out into the country to fight for imperial preference or remaining a member of a Government which in theory was prepared to implement a watered-down version of his policy and in practice was liable to dilute the contents still further for the sake of self-preservation. He chose to resign. The Cabinet meeting was due to take place on the afternoon of Monday, 14 September. Balfour had only the weekend to decide on his tactics. It was no longer within his power to avoid a crisis. All he could do was to arrange matters in such a way as to give the Government the best possible chance of surviving its term of office. He sincerely believed that a policy based on the freedom to retaliate against foreign tariffs was best suited to the mood of the Party and the constituencies. Chamberlain's offer gave him the opportunity of abandoning the food tax and preference, but the inevitable repercussions might assume serious proportions if his resignation was interpreted as a free trade victory. The only way round the problem was to ensure that the extremist free-traders, Hamilton and Ritchie in particular, accompanied the Colonial Secretary to the back benches. Balfour might then appear not as one who was out of sympathy with fiscal reform, but as the champion of the compromise solution (**28, 30, 33, 42, 67**).

Immediately before the Cabinet meeting the Prime Minister had a long conversation with Chamberlain. Balfour accepted his resignation and persuaded him to use his influence to prevent his

son, Austen, who shared his father's views on fiscal policy, from
following his example. He made it known that he intended the
younger Chamberlain to replace Ritchie as Chancellor. The remainder of the Cabinet did not know of these latest developments. Nor were
they enlightened during the subsequent discussions. Balfour argued
later that there was no useful purpose to be served by confusing the
main issue with matters which could not 'affect the opinion of those
Members of the Cabinet who were not prepared heartily to accept
a change of fiscal policy at all'.

It is difficult to believe that any but his fondest admirers were
prepared to accept his side of the story. Setting aside the fact that
the Cabinet had a right to be informed of the decisions (Balfour
had taken good care to allow himself a loophole by not officially
replying to Chamberlain's communication), it was by no means
certain that events would have followed the same course had the
free-traders known the facts.

Hamilton's account of the meeting clearly reveals that his resignation was based on the assumption that Balfour was not prepared
to forsake the Colonial Secretary [**doc. 10**].

There was a further meeting on the 15th and when the Cabinet
dispersed the free-traders found an early opportunity to meet
privately. Ritchie and Hamilton decided to send in their resignations
immediately, and they assumed that Devonshire and Burleigh
would follow their example within 'a day or so'. Their letters to the
Prime Minister (dated 15 September) expressed disapproval of
imperial preference and tariff retaliation, but a personal communication to Balfour written on the same day by Devonshire leaves no
doubt that it was food taxation which tipped the scales [**doc. 11**].
In the evening the Duke, having failed to obtain from the Prime
Minister satisfactory reassurances on the matter of food taxation,
decided to offer his resignation. He failed to notice, or chose to
ignore, a hint that the job of Colonial Secretary might soon be
vacant [**doc. 12**].

The following day, when Balfour was safely in possession of the
letters from Hamilton and Ritchie (Burleigh's resignation arrived
shortly afterwards), he called Devonshire and informed him that
Chamberlain was to leave the Government. Despite the uncompromising attitude which the Duke had adopted not twenty-four
hours earlier, he agreed, after some discussion, to withdraw his
resignation. Not unreasonably he asked that his three colleagues

should have the opportunity of reconsidering their position. This was the last thing Balfour was prepared to do, and the unfortunate Devonshire, whose sense of propriety was torn between loyalty to the free-traders and a desire to save the Party from internecine disputes, was flattered and cajoled into accepting his terms. There could be no parley with the three Ministers who had proved themselves to be irreconcilable (**28, 33, 40**).

8 Tory Disaster

The delegates to the annual conference of the National Union of Conservative and Constitutional Associations gathered at Sheffield on 1 October. The highlight of the proceedings was the Prime Minister's address which was intended to rally support for his leadership.

Chamberlain's followers, led by Howard Vincent and Henry Chaplin, were in a majority at the Conference and during the early stages of the fiscal debate it seemed likely they would be able to secure a resolution supporting preference. But if the free-traders and tariff reformers agreed on nothing else, they both recognised the need for some compromise that would keep the Conservative Government in power. Balfour earned a cool reception when he outlined his policy: 'My request . . . to you tonight . . . is that the people of this country should give to the Government of this country, from whatever party that Government may be drawn, that freedom of [trade] negotiation of which we have been deprived' (5).

Somebody in the hall shouted, 'How can we give you that power?' The speaker sidetracked the question but the audience recognised the implication. No positive action could be expected, even within the limited framework of Balfour's policy, until the electorate had delivered its verdict. Fortunately, for Balfour, the urgent need for Party discipline was reluctantly acknowledged. Without a sign of enthusiasm the conference unanimously resolved to thank the Prime Minister for instituting an enquiry into the fiscal system and to welcome his intention of securing fiscal freedom in the negotiations and commercial relations with foreign countries.

If Balfour experienced a sense of elation after his victory at Sheffield, it was quickly dispelled by the news of Devonshire's resignation from the Cabinet. After a brief period of reflection the Duke had come to realise that his position was untenable. He did not relish the prospect of appearing in the history books as the Judas of the free-traders, and to preserve his reputation as an honest politician he sought desperately for an excuse that would enable him to follow the example of his friends and abandon his ministerial career. The Sheffield declaration gave him his only opportunity. It omitted, he said, 'a definite statement of adherence to the principles of free trade'.

Balfour replied immediately and made no attempt to disguise his bitter disappointment: 'To resign now, and to resign on the speech, is to take the course most calculated to make yet harder the hard task of the peace makers' (**25**).

It is difficult to feel much sympathy for Balfour. He was prepared to play an artful game, hoping to bolster up his Government with the prestige of an elder statesman who appeared to lack the confidence of his own opinions. He lost, and he had no one but himself to blame.

The vacancies in the Cabinet were filled during the week following the conference. Austen Chamberlain was appointed Chancellor of the Exchequer—a promotion which met with general approval even in the ranks of the free-traders. Balfour had hoped that Lord Milner would become Colonial Secretary but the offer was refused. Chamberlain's successor turned out be a far less exciting character, a lawyer MP who had worked with Milner during the last stages of the war in South Africa. Alfred Lyttleton had not previously served as a minister.

'It is now at least a Protectionist Government', wrote Hicks-Beach, 'without the courage for a Protectionist policy' (**35**).

The Government survived for two years—far longer than anyone expected—and for the most of that time Balfour managed to keep his ministers on a tight rein. He provided the means, probably the only means, of holding together the opposing forces within the Conservative Party.

Unfortunately, the Prime Minister's fiscal policy was not a vote winner. Jet black and snow white are easier colours to distinguish than pale grey. For many of the electorate, the only alternative to pure free trade was complete protection. In the constituencies it was Chamberlain not Balfour who made the running on the tariff question. On 6 October 1903, 6,000 people packed St Andrews Hall in Glasgow to hear the first speech of Chamberlain's tariff reform campaign. He spoke with all the fervour of a dedicated preacher and his enthusiasm for the general concept of a united Empire excited his admirers who crowded the platform. But he committed a serious error of judgment. Referring to the 'substantial advantage' which the colonies were prepared to offer in return for preference, he firmly asserted: 'They will reserve to us the trade which we already enjoy. They will not arrange their tariffs in future in order to start industries in competition with those which are already in existence in the mother country.'

All the years he spent at the Colonial Office had not taught him that the nationalistic ambition of the colonies did not allow for subservience to Britain. There was cheering in St Andrew's Hall but not a whisper of an echo from the dominions. When the corrected version of the speech was published the phrase 'much, at any rate of', was inserted before the words, 'the trade which we already enjoy'. The next sentence was omitted but, as if to underline the fact that Chamberlain's illusions were not entirely destroyed, his appeal to the colonies remained unamended. 'There are many things which you do not now make, many things for which we have a great capacity of production. Leave them to us as you have left them hitherto.'

This was the first but not the last time that Chamberlain embarrassed his lieutenants by voicing extravagant claims. His arguments were often supported by inaccurate or misleading statistics which left the tariff reformers open to serious attack. When, towards the end of the year, he managed to survive a number of speeches without needing to retract a single sentence, *Punch* reported that 'doctors are not without a certain amount of uneasiness, Mr Chamberlain not having eaten a single word for days'.

The opposition was got under way by an attack from Asquith who embarked on his own extensive campaign with a speech at Cinderford. His efforts were supplemented by the activities of countless Liberal politicians who eagerly fastened upon an objective for which they could fight as a united team. It was not long before the Unionist free-traders were also involved in the struggle. But for the moment Balfour was less worried by the Free Trade League than by his ex-ministers who wanted to explain to the electorate their reasons for disrupting the Government. Hamilton, Ritchie and Devonshire wrote to the Prime Minister requesting permission to make reference to the Cabinet proceedings which led to their resignations. Balfour gave his approval (he had little choice), but urged them not to disclose confidential information. His appeal was only partly successful and he was subsequently embarrassed by their attempts to clear themselves of the responsibility for the recent crisis; in particular by Hamilton's statement to his constituents which clearly indicated that right up until the last moment the Party leader was in favour of some measure of imperial preference.

Moderate free-traders were appalled by the prospect of a split vote which would guarantee victory to the Liberals in the general election. Diehards like Winston Churchill were openly advocating a free trade alliance with the Liberals, and Devonshire was in active consultation with the Opposition leaders.

All the signs pointed to a Liberal victory in the general election and Campbell-Bannerman was not particularly worried when the Conservative free-traders abandoned the idea of a formal Lib-Con alliance. Before long seven of the best known free-traders including Winston Churchill crossed the floor of the House. In 1906 the Liberals gave a free run to three Conservatives who supported them not only on the fiscal question but also on such issues as education, alien immigration and the importation of Chinese labour into South Africa (**48**).

The anti-Conservative swing recorded in a series of by-elections in 1903 and early 1904 failed to discourage the tariff reformers, who blamed the Government for not giving a strong lead on imperial preference. The propaganda campaign was stepped up and thousands of leaflets and posters were distributed from their headquarters in Victoria Street. Balfour's idea of a fiscal enquiry was taken over by Chamberlain, who adapted the scheme to suit his own purposes. Early in the new year he announced the formation of a Tariff Commission. It consisted of a representative selection of businessmen whose purpose was to investigate the conditions in which British industry had to operate and to recommend how tariffs might be used to stimulate production, discourage unfair competition and develop imperial trade.

Meanwhile the Government majority fell to forty-six on a vote taken at the end of a fiscal debate on 9 March. When it was known that the Opposition intended to move a free trade resolution, Balfour allowed an amendment to go forward in the name of J. L. Wharton, the Conservative member for Ripon. It approved 'the explicit declaration of His Majesty's Ministers that their policy of fiscal reform does not include either a general system of Protection or Preference based on the taxation of food' (**63**). But the tariff reformers (who were in a two to one majority over the free-traders)

71

could not accept the terms of the amendment without admitting a serious defeat and at a meeting prior to the debate they forced Balfour to back down. The result was that some free-traders voted for the Government because they could not bear to support the Liberals, while others abstained. Both sections accused each other of disloyalty.

With this split the Free Food League could not survive. In November the Duke of Devonshire proposed that the League should be disbanded.

Debates and questions on fiscal reform occupied a higher proportion of the 1904 Parliamentary timetable than any other subject. The Opposition attack centred on Balfour who was accused of engineering a secret pact with Chamberlain. They argued he was disguising his real intentions for the sake of retaining power for himself and his party, and at the first opportunity his Government would implement a scheme of imperial preference. Don't trust him, cried the Liberals, whatever he says now he means to tax your food.

The chief evidence was supplied by Lord George Hamilton, who revealed that during the crisis meetings of August 1903 the Cabinet examined two documents, one advocating tariff retaliation, the other imperial preference. Opposition pressure forced the Government to admit that the second document, the Blue Paper, was not a product of Hamilton's imagination. At the same time Balfour refused to publish it because it was a confidential Cabinet memorandum (**30, 33**).

The attempt to brand the Prime Minister as a tariff reform sympathiser pleased Chamberlain and his friends who, by this time, were strong enough to claim recognition and official backing. By June 1904 by-election defeats and defections to the Liberals had reduced the Government majority from 168 to just under 100. Since those members committed to Chamberlain numbered over 100 they were capable of forcing a dissolution at any time.

There was no longer any serious reason for Balfour to worry about the free-traders but he was still left with the problem of holding the balance between opposing forces. On one hand were the extreme tariff reformers and on the other those members who favoured a less ambitious experiment in protection. Partly to avoid the sneer that he lacked the courage of his own convictions but more particularly to pacify the tariff reformers who constantly challenged him to give a lead, Balfour tried a new approach to the imperial question.

During the summer he engaged in long discussion with Austen Chamberlain who was the tariff reformers' chief spokesman in the Government. They were unable to reach agreement but the Chancellor of the Exchequer was encouraged by the Prime Minister's readiness to negotiate. In late August he delivered a strong appeal, setting out the minimum concessions which he believed were necessary to secure a lasting settlement. Balfour was willing to accept his chief proposal that if the Conservative Government was returned to power at the next election it should immediately summon a colonial conference to discuss imperial preference. But he made one stipulation. Before any action could be taken on the recommendations of the conference the voters had to be given another chance to record their verdict. This was his 'two elections' scheme which he introduced to the public on 3 October at a meeting in Edinburgh.

Austen Chamberlain objected strenuously. What possible useful purpose could be served by a second election? He angrily concluded that it was simply an attempt to pacify the free-traders.

Joseph Chamberlain's comments were more generous than those of his son. He described the proposal to hold a second election as the only blemish in a plan which otherwise 'marks a great advance in the programme of the Unionist Party'. He argued that if a Government pledged to deal with the colonial questions was elected with a large majority it would be inconvenient to ask for a nation-wide vote of confidence after only a short period in office. On the other hand, if the appeal was delayed for two or three years the popularity of the Government might have waned for reasons which had nothing to do with preference or tariffs.

He wrote to Balfour suggesting they should meet to discuss the situation. The Prime Minister accepted the invitation. It was only the second occasion in the eighteen months since Chamberlain resigned office that the two leaders had agreed to talk together about the future policy of the Party. Not unexpectedly the second election was the main topic of conversation. Chamberlain was unable to make much headway with his counterproposals and on the day following the meeting, Balfour wrote him a summary of the reasons for his refusal to abandon the Edinburgh plan. He argued that without the promise of a second election they could not even begin to hope for a *free* colonial conference. If Chamberlain had his way delegates from home and abroad would have to make all sorts of guarantees to their electors before they started their discussions and the result would be the same as for all previous imperial conferences —no agreement on anything really worth while. On the other hand, if the delegates attended the negotiations without any instructions from their voters, on condition that the final scheme would be submitted for their approval, then, Balfour claimed, there was a real chance of producing a scheme that would involve concessions on both sides and yet have a wide appeal because it held out the prospect of rapid economic growth and closer imperial cooperation on trade matters.

Chamberlain, by reputation a man of business and action, was in fact far too much of an idealist to appreciate Balfour's hardheaded realism. He believed that it was the responsibility of Britain to summon a colonial conference and to submit to the representatives detailed proposals which would then form a basis for discussion. Balfour was more concerned with the problem of creating a favourable atmosphere for the tariff negotiations by avoiding commitments.

Chamberlain was under the impression that his campaign had achieved that particular object. But he sadly overestimated his support in the country which came chiefly from powerful sectional interests who were more attracted to the benefits of protection than to the ideals of empire unity. The mass of the working-class voters were bitterly opposed to food taxation.

There were, however, two serious defects in Balfour's election strategy. First, like most of his policy statements, it was too sophisticated for the average voter to appreciate. Even Joseph Chamberlain, who for several months had the benefit of the Prime Minister's personal tuition, was forced to admit: 'I do not sufficiently understand your scheme at present to speak with sufficient knowledge upon it!' (**1**). Secondly, the leading members of the party were more or less reconciled to a Liberal victory at the general election, a contingency for which the Balfour plan did not cater. If their pessimism was justified by the results and the 'two elections' pledge was not rescinded, tariff reform could be delayed indefinitely. Some members on both sides of the House assumed that this was precisely the Prime Minister's intention and Austen Chamberlain urged upon him the need to avoid misinterpretation by reconsidering his tactics.

Balfour insisted he had no intention of avoiding his obligations. He was bound by the terms of the Edinburgh speech which, he believed, constituted the best means of securing a solution to the trade problem. According to Austen Chamberlain, if the Conservatives were defeated at the general election, Balfour agreed to think again about the 'two elections' plan but that was the only concession the tariff reformers were able to acquire. The Opposition and the public were not informed of the amendment to the official policy. No one in the Conservative Party was eager to provide the Liberals with more ammunition by openly discussing the possibility of a change of government.

The Chamberlains realised that they had pushed Balfour as far as he would go. There was nothing more they could do except continue the job of educating the voters. For his part, the Prime Minister attended to the business of preparing the ground for the Colonial Conference which was due to meet in 1906. In December 1904 he and Lyttleton drafted a circular dispatch to the governors of the dominions which proposed that the conference should henceforth be known as the Imperial Council with 'a body in permanent existence to which the Imperial Council at their meetings could refer questions for subsequent examination and report'.

> [This] Commission would only act upon references made either by the Imperial Council at their meetings, or by any two or more of the Governments concerned by agreement at any time, and its function would of course be of a purely consultative and advisory character. It would have the usual powers of Royal Commissions to take evidence and call for documents (1).

It was apparent that Balfour intended the Commission to be the main instrument in the negotiation of a new tariff structure.

Meanwhile the remaining Conservative free-traders were hounded by their protectionist opponents who demanded nothing less than their complete destruction. In the key constituencies the Tariff Reform League encouraged the formation of rival associations whose purpose was to undermine the authority of the sitting members and if possible to oust them in favour of representatives who were prepared to give their allegiance to Chamberlain.

The publicity department organised demonstrations and meetings and the distribution of literature on a generous scale. To stimulate the support of the poorer sections of the community the intricacies of imperial preference were reduced to slogans and simple messages which the uninformed voter could appreciate without difficulty.

Each night during the Norwich by-election campaign, lantern slides were displayed in the market place and one of the regular speakers was made up to look like Chamberlain.

Elsewhere, postcard-sized reproductions of political cartoons were handed out at meetings and pushed through letterboxes. In one example, a ragged cloth-capped worker, clasping in one hand a loaf of bread bitterly complains, 'To tell you the truth I am almost tired of this "Big Loaf". I want something more than cheap bread and promises.' A tariff reformer in the image of a jolly-faced John Bull character who carries a loaded basket of meat and poultry voices a happier refrain. 'What is $\frac{1}{4}d$ more for a 4 lb loaf when I have money left after marketing.'

The working class remained unimpressed by propaganda and gimmickry but the businessmen and the squirearchy who were the backbone of the League exercised a strong personal influence on their home ground and in constituencies represented by free-trade unionists they were usually strong enough to make political life uncomfortable and hazardous. As one of the chief spokesmen for the free-traders in the House of Commons, Lord Hugh Cecil, MP for Greenwich, was considered a strategic target by Chamberlain's guerrilla fighters. A local branch of the Tariff Reform League was established in his constituency early in 1904 and before long they gained a majority on the executive council of the local Conservative Association. In February 1905 Cecil was asked to resign.

Fortunately for the free-traders he was no ordinary backbencher. Lord Hugh Cecil was nationally acknowledged as a rising star in the Conservative Party and his reputation was enhanced by his family connections. He was the fifth son of Lord Salisbury and the Prime Minister's cousin. On Balfour's instructions the Chief Whip notified the Greenwich Association that the Party would not withdraw its support from Hugh Cecil. Chamberlain was furious and when the tariff reformers nominated Hamilton Benn, a local Tory leader, to fight their cause at the general election he endorsed their decision and declared 'that the majority of the Unionist party, whether in Greenwich or elsewhere are not only justified, but are required by their duty in a matter so urgent and important to make every effort to have their opinions fully represented in the House of Commons after the next election'.

Balfour's intervention put heart into the free-traders. But if they anticipated that he would exert himself on behalf of hard-pressed members who were not his relations they were soon to be disappointed. After Greenwich he refused to participate in constituency squabbles, a policy motivated, as he frankly admitted, by an antipathy towards the free-traders who had caused him considerable trouble during the early stages of the controversy, had constantly rejected his advice, and had proved to be more intractable in the House of Commons than the extreme tariff reformers. 'They first embarrass me by opposition,' he complained, 'and then by demands for assistance.'

At the beginning of 1905 at least twenty-four free-traders were defending their constituencies against a takeover bid by Chamberlain's supporters. Eighteen of these members had voted against the Government's fiscal policy on at least one occasion during the 1904 session. It may appear unreasonable that the other six, who loyally supported the Prime Minister in the division lobbies, should have suffered attacks from a Conservative organisation which also claimed to support the Government. Part of the trouble was the absence of any clear dividing line between the free-traders and those who gave their allegiance to Balfour. A proportion of the first group (including Lord Hugh Cecil) was prepared to tolerate some measure of retaliation against excessive foreign tariffs, and within such limits to allow preferential entry to colonial products.

But from the point of view of the tariff reformers, the free-traders who were in the Government camp were just as dangerous as those who declared outright opposition to Balfour. Both sections were fighting to preserve as much as possible of the traditional fiscal policy. The situation was made even more confusing when the Tariff Reform League set up branches in constituencies where the members were in no way burdened by free trade principles but simply preferred Balfour's leadership to that of Chamberlain. In these cases the League was not usually motivated by a sinister political aim. Its purpose was to exert pressure on the associations to adopt a more radical approach to the question of international trade.

Between January 1904 and December 1905 there were twenty-eight by-elections in Conservative controlled constituencies. Fourteen seats were lost to the Opposition.

With no sign of an improvement in the voting figures, the question which dominated Cabinet discussions was the date of the general election. Everyone recognised the probability of a Government defeat. The tariff reform controversy had irreparably damaged the prestige of the party and there were other factors at work which lengthened still further the odds against victory. The Education and the Licensing Bills and the decision to import some 50,000 Chinese labourers to work the South African gold mines aroused the Non-conformist conscience and contributed to the revival of Liberal Party morale, while the Taff Vale judgment stimulated the Labour movement. Both parties were able to take strong electoral advantage of the protection issue.

During the summer recess Austen Chamberlain urged on the Prime Minister the need for an early resignation as opposed to a dissolution of Parliament. In this way Campbell-Bannerman would be forced to set up a minority government at least for the period until an election could be arranged, and there was a fair chance that his parliamentary contingent, divided on policy (particularly Home Rule for Ireland) and leadership, would prove themselves unfit to rule. But Sir Alexander Acland-Hood, the Conservative Chief Whip, argued against the resignation plan. He believed Campbell-Bannerman would refuse to take office and Balfour would be forced to carry on 'with all the discredit of having tried to run away, having been caught and brought back in disgrace' (**55**). Much to the disappointment of the tariff reformers Balfour decided to postpone his decision until the end of the year.

Chamberlain was particularly concerned with the state of party morale in the constituencies and believed that further delay would seriously weaken the organisation. But most of the MPs, agents and constituency chairmen favoured a policy of 'wait and see'.

As the year progressed the Government's hold on power gradually weakened. In 1905 the Liberals snatched seven seats from their opponents. Their campaign to attract the support of the Unionist free trade electors was assisted by Chamberlain, who frequently and deliberately asserted that there was practically no difference between his policy and that advocated by Balfour. In November the delegates to the annual conference voted overwhelmingly in favour of tariff reform and the Prime Minister's appeal for moderation and unity was answered a few days later when Chamberlain addressed the Liberal Unionist Council.

> You must not [he said] ask the majority, be it nine-tenths or, as I think, ninety-nine hundredths, to sacrifice their convictions to the prejudices of the minority. No army was ever led success-

fully to battle on the principle that the lamest man should govern the march of the army. I say you must not go into the battle which is impending with blunted swords merely in order to satisfy the scruples of those who do not wish to fight at all (**30**).

It was obvious that the party divisions were as wide and deep as they had ever been and the Prime Minister was disinclined to carry his burden any further. His majority, which in 1900 stood at 134, had fallen to 68. The Liberals had gained 24 seats in a series of by-election victories and 9 Conservatives had crossed the floor of the House. The survival of the Government depended upon the good-will of less than 40 members and even the small and demoralised group of free-traders were able to raise that many votes. Sooner or later the Opposition were bound to win a major division on a fiscal motion and Balfour had no intention of waiting to experience the final humiliation. On 4 December he resigned.

The following day Sir Henry Campbell-Bannerman was invited by the King to form a new administration. The expectation that the Liberals would be unable to assume office without publicising their differences on Home Rule and the Irish question was soon proved to be hopelessly misplaced. The takeover was smooth and confident, and the Conservatives were left in a position where they had to explain to the electorate why it was necessary for them to be returned to power when, on their own admission, they were incapable of performing their duties.

The election campaign opened almost immediately. Voting was to begin on 12 January but the full results were not expected until early February, when the last constituencies went to the polls. Throughout the period of the campaign the Conservatives were burdened by a deep mood of pessimism. Balfour concentrated on the shortcomings of his opponents and somehow overlooked the need to provide an alternative programme. Even Chamberlain, in his address to his constituents, gave greater attention to Home Rule than to fiscal reform. But however hard they tried to open an attack on the new Government, the Liberals soon put them back on the defensive by focusing public attention on three main issues—education, Chinese 'slavery' and tariff reform. Of these, tariff reform was unquestionably the most important. It cropped up in the election addresses of nearly all the candidates. Platform speakers were obsessed by it. For the Liberals, it was the signal for spontaneous excitement and elation. For the Conservatives, it was the cause of utter despair.

The number of constituencies where Conservative tariff reformers and free-traders fought in opposition to each other was remarkably small: a total of not more than fifteen. Eleven of the seats were contested by Liberals who won seven of them on a split Conservative vote. After the first few days of voting it was clear that Campbell-Bannerman's Government would enjoy a massive victory. On ˅2 January Ipswich turned out both its Conservative members. Immediately attention was focused on the North Country where Arthur Balfour was standing for re-election in East Manchester, the home of free trade. Two days before the poll he received a good luck message from his cousin Robert Cecil, who hoped that 'there is no serious risk in East Manchester. For you to be defeated and for Joe to get in would be in my view the greatest electoral disaster that could occur to us' (**1**).

He did not have to wait long for the news. On the 13th he learned that Balfour was out. In Manchester and Salford, the Conservatives lost all eight seats. Lancashire and the West Riding followed the same pattern with every constituency except Wigan returning Liberal or Labour members. There was no doubt that the textile industry regarded free trade as the best guarantee of cheap supplies of cotton.

On the Monday there were more Liberal gains including Central Leeds (Gerald Balfour's constituency) and Rochester, the centre of the depressed cement industry. Some of the best known tariff reformers, including Vicary Gibbs, Sir Vincent Caillard and Sir Howard Vincent, were up for election in the Sheffield and Bradford areas, where commercial interests complained bitterly of the hardships caused by the dumping of foreign imports. Of the big names, Howard Vincent was the only one to survive. He managed to hang on to Sheffield Central, where he was opposed by Stanley Udale, the Chairman of the Liberals Free Trade Union. Henry Chaplin was not so lucky. At Sleaford he was turned out in favour of a Liberal anti-vaccinationist. The chain of disasters stretched to London, Scotland and the rural constituencies. Birmingham remained loyal to the Unionists, but even here the Liberals mounted a powerful attack against Chamberlain's electoral machine.

When the final results came in, the Liberals had won 400 seats and the Irish Nationalists 83. The growing demand for social reform was reflected in the return of 30 Labour members, 25 of whom benefited from an electoral pact with the Liberals. The Conservatives were reduced to a minority of 157 and their share of the total vote fell from 51.1 to 43.6 per cent (**21**). A political correspondent of *The Times* calculated that Chamberlain commanded the allegiance of 109 members against 32 who had pledged themselves not to go beyond Balfour's programme. The remainder were either diehard free traders or possible supporters of retaliation. These figures, compiled only as a rough guide to the state of the Party, contained several inaccuracies but they showed clearly that Chamberlain was in control of a majority in the Parliamentary Party.

In some quarters it was taken for granted that Balfour would be ousted from the leadership. But his only possible contender was exhausted by the campaign and in no mood to take advantage of his opportunity. A Conservative stronghold, the City of London constituency, was made available for the ex-Prime Minister, who spent much of his time prior to the by-election negotiating with the tariff reformers. Correspondence relating to fiscal policy between Chamberlain and Balfour was published on 14 February 1906. The Valentine letters informed the public that tariff reform was the 'first constructive work of the Unionist Party'. Balfour proposed and Chamberlain accepted a plan by which a future Conservative government would be entitled to impose a moderate general tariff on manufactured goods and a small duty on foreign corn for the purpose of establishing 'more equal terms of competition for British trade' and 'closer commercial union with the Colonies'. It was also acknowledged that a general tariff might prove to be a necessary source of additional Exchequer revenue [**doc. 13**].

The electorate were unimpressed. Balfour was speaking on behalf not of a Government but a weak and demoralised Opposition. He was powerless to implement his policy and the concessions to the tariff reformers which were hedged with 'ifs' and 'buts' made very little impact on party members who clearly recognised that the fiscal question was no longer a live political issue. Early in the new parliamentary session a free trade resolution was introduced by a Liberal whose intention was to embarrass the Opposition spokesmen. The exercise was entirely successful. Balfour launched into a long and crudite address which evoked from the normally indecisive Campbell-Bannerman a brutal and dogmatic attack on the protectionists. 'I say, enough of this foolery! It might have answered very well in the last Parliament, but it is altogether out of place in this Parliament. The tone and temper of this Parliament will not permit it. Move your amendments and let us get to business.'

The honourable members did just that.

9 Victory for Protection

During the election, and at a time when it was obvious that the Liberals were heading for a massive victory, Balfour was quoted as saying: 'the great Unionist Party should still control, whether in power or whether in opposition, the destinies of this great Empire.' There was only one possible interpretation of these words. Balfour expected the House of Lords, with its permanent Conservative majority, to vote down any radical legislation. The policy did not prevent the Government from achieving an impressive record for social reform but some of the Liberals' most favoured proposals were defeated, delayed or severely amended by the Upper House. The conflict between the Lords and the Commons dominated politics up to 1910 and diverted public attention from the serious differences that still existed within the Conservative Party on the place of tariff reform in official policy (**39**).

Despite his agreement with Chamberlain, Balfour made few public references to 'the first constructive work of the Unionist Party'. Dedicated tariff reformers or 'whole hoggers' to use their popular label, suspected that the party leader was taking advantage of Chamberlain's declining health and energy (he suffered a heart attack in July 1906) to retreat from his earlier commitments. 'What we really require', wrote Austen Chamberlain, 'is that he should follow up the letter of February 14th by speech and action, and that his speech should emphasise the need for action and not the qualifications—the "ifs" and "thoughs" and so forth of that letter' (**56**).

The idea appalled Balfour, who believed that the sole duty of the Opposition was to oppose. Any detailed promises on his part would merely allow the Government to escape the responsibility of defending their actions by indulging in the more pleasurable business of attacking Conservative plans [**doc. 14**]. In any case, the old divisions within his Party still existed, however depleted its parliamentary ranks, and Balfour's duty, as he saw it, was to hold the ring by continuing to play his traditional role of the benevolent neutral. But with the threat of yet another tariff reform revolt Balfour devoted a major speech to the subject of imperial preference early in 1907, at the same time warning his audience: 'If we become a party of one idea we shall fail to carry even that idea to any successful conclusion.'

It was unfair to the whole hoggers to suggest that protection was their sole political object. Imperial preference was naturally at the head of their list of priorities but they hoped, as Austen Chamberlain frequently pointed out, to use the revenue from tariffs to finance a Conservative programme of social reform. The Liberals, pledged to free trade, were compelled to raise taxation to provide for such expensive measures as a national scheme of old age pensions. How much more attractive to the voters if the money could be raised painlessly, or apparently so. This was the policy originally advocated by Joseph Chamberlain in the early days of the imperial preference campaign. He abandoned the idea when he discovered that working-class voters favoured increases in direct taxes (which were paid largely by the wealthier sections of the community) instead of tariffs. Now Conservative MPs and constituency leaders, realising that further social reform was inevitable, were prepared to take another shot at persuading the electorate to accept import duties. They were in a better position than Joseph Chamberlain to produce statistics and arguments showing that tariffs would bring all sorts of advantages to the working class without having any appreciable effect on the cost of living.

The tariff reformers also gained strength within the Party by their policy of hounding those members who remained loyal to free trade principles (**16**). By 1909 they were in complete control of the Party. Balfour recognised their dominance by showing, for him, unusual enthusiasm for protectionist policy and the Central Office refused to endorse any candidate who would not support imperial preference. A trade recession in 1907–8 and growing unemployment helped to build up support in the country.

At the Imperial Conference of 1907 the dominion prime ministers, led by Alfred Deakin of Australia, campaigned hard for imperial preference. He showed his contempt for free trade Liberals by turning down a Government offer of a privy councillorship. It was an encouraging time for the Chamberlains who optimistically looked forward to the next election.

Then came the 'People's Budget'. It was presented by Lloyd George, the Welsh lawyer who had succeeded to the job of Chancellor of the Exchequer with a reputation as one of the most fearsome of the radical reformers. His proposals included a tax increase of $1s$ to $1s$ $2d$ in the £ on incomes exceeding £3,000 a year, a super-tax of $6d$ in the £ on incomes above £5,000, and higher death duties. Such impositions, apparently so mild, shocked Conservative thinkers, but the Chancellor also had his eye on another enemy. He calculated, correctly, as it turned out, that the House of Lords would throw out the Budget. It was a hazardous decision for the peers to take. On only a single previous occasion since 1688 had they challenged the Commons' right to legislate on matters involving expenditure or taxation. Their action was bound to create sympathy for the elected Government and it was not at all surprising that Asquith, who had taken over as Prime Minister when Campbell-Bannerman retired in 1908, decided to submit the dispute to the judgment of the voters. Parliament was dissolved on 10 January 1910.

Tariff reform figured prominently in the election addresses of most Conservative candidates. It was offered as an alternative means of raising revenue for social reform, a method of safeguarding national industries against foreign state-aided competition and the only possible hope of developing trade within the Empire.

When the votes were counted the overall result was a disappointment to all the contenders. The Government lost nearly a third of their constituencies, but the Conservatives lost the election and Asquith resumed his leadership with the aid of Labour and Irish Nationalist support.

Within a year there was another general election, this time to seek approval for a measure to curb the powers of the House of Lords. The other major issue of this campaign was Home Rule for Ireland, which was pledged by Asquith in return for parliamentary backing from the Irish members but desperately opposed by the Opposition who believed that independence for a part of the United Kingdom would be the prelude to the collapse of the Empire. Tariff Reform was almost forgotten except when a Conservative proposal for a referendum to settle differences between Lords and Commons was neatly countered by Asquith, who asked if they would submit food taxes to a direct vote of the people. Balfour accepted the challenge and without consulting his colleagues announced his readiness to hold a referendum on tariff reform. Austen Chamberlain, who was now chief spokesman for the protectionists described his leader's action as 'a slap in the face' but he should not have been surprised at Balfour's enthusiasm for what amounted to a 'double election'. For the moment, however, he did not have to worry about the practical implications. The election was close run but the Liberals again scraped back into power with the assistance of their Labour and Irish allies (**29**).

The tariff reformers had missed their chance and though Balfour was not to blame for their defeat—his embarrassing referendum pledge almost certainly won more votes than it lost—he was the natural scapegoat and resigned in November. Most observers expected Austen Chamberlain to take over but, like his father, he was thought to be too much of a maverick to be trusted with the leadership. It was another tariff reformer who satisfied the Conservative need for confident respectability. Andrew Bonar Law, son of an Ulster Presbyterian minister, born in Canada and raised in Scotland, succeeded to the job of restoring his Party's control over the country.

Even the most ardent tariff reformers were depressed by their failure to put across their case in two elections and there was a general feeling in the Party that protection should be pushed to the background of politics, at least for the time being.

Bonar Law made a few cautious references to imperial preference and then, in December 1912, unexpectedly back-pedalled on the question of food taxes. He announced that when the Conservatives regained power import duties in this sector of the economy were to be limited to wheat, meat, and possibly dairy produce. Furthermore, the duties would not be introduced until after an Imperial Conference had signified they were essential for a general scheme of preference. His attempt to make food taxes more palatable to the voter almost caused a rebellion among the more dedicated tariff reformers who thought they were dealing with a second Balfour. This half-hearted approach was not the way to gain the support of the dominions. Bonar Law refused to change his policy and for a time he seriously considered resigning the leadership. But another party split would have helped only the Liberals and for the sake of unity he was persuaded to keep his job (**14**).

A Tory club called the Round Table, organised by a group of imperialists who had worked with Milner in South Africa, tried to keep alive the ideal of Empire unity, but their grandiose schemes were reminiscent of the days when a federal parliament was seriously considered and by this time every practical politician knew enough to avoid wasting time with such fairytale notions.

In 1912 a Dominions Royal Commission was set up to study the possibilities of Empire development. Its terms of reference were limited by a veto on recommendations that could affect the fiscal policy of any government of the Empire, thus excluding imperial preference; but the tariff reformers anticipated that the report would help to keep public interest alive until the Conservatives were returned to power.

Events did not turn out quite the way they expected. The arms race in Europe and the dismal recitation of international crises that led to the outbreak of the first world war introduced a new order of political priorities. The work of this Royal Commission was thought to be of minor value while the country was in a state of emergency, and it was not until 1917 that the report was eventually published. It recommended the setting up of an Imperial Development Board (an idea first proposed by Alfred Deakin as early as 1907), the functions of which were to include:

Watching and reporting upon the changing requirements of the Empire in respect of materials and commodities, and to mature plans for promoting and improving their production within the Empire;
Investigating in collaboration with existing institutions and committees for scientific research . . . the possibilities of production within the Empire of such of these essential materials and commodities as now are, or may in the future be found to be, mainly produced and controlled outside its limits, as well as the possibilities of new supplies generally.
Considering and devising means for the direction of Empire capital towards the development of Empire resources;
Studying the larger aspects of migration within the Empire with a view to securing and maintaining a sufficiency of population in all its parts. (**18**).

While not particularly exciting in itself the report came at just the right time to help influence the Government (by now a coalition of Liberal, Conservative and Labour members, led by Lloyd George) in the direction of a fundamental change in trade policy. Two years previously, Reginald McKenna, Chancellor of the Exchequer, had

87

introduced into his Budget an element of protection by imposing duties at the rate of 33⅓ per cent *ad valorem* on luxury articles such as motor cars, motor cycles, clocks and watches.

The aim here was to save valuable shipping space by cutting down on non-essential imports. Duties on tea, sugar, coffee, cocoa and tobacco that were non-protective because they did not affect home industry were increased by an average of 50 per cent as part of a general plan to raise the money to fight the costliest war in history. McKenna insisted that his measures were intended only for the duration of the emergency (**59**):

> No fiscal principle of any kind is compromised by the present proposals. . . . We can, then, on both sides, allow our opinions upon principle (which is left entirely untouched) to remain in abeyance. When once again we have peace, and once again the taxes must come up to be reconsidered, then will be the time for us to argue about the basis of fiscal theory. . . . We have deliberately abandoned theory in the special circumstances of the War.

No one had time to argue with him.

In 1916 allied representatives met in Paris to discuss, among other economic matters, the principle of ensuring that in future they would not be dependent on enemy countries for material and manufactures of a kind essential to their normal commercial activities.

In one sense this was rather like shutting the stable door after the cavalry had bolted. Britain had caused herself a lot of worry by allowing prewar Germany to control the supply of ingredients for certain munitions and to dominate the production of some essential manufactures such as optical and electrical instruments. But even though those problems belonged to the past the government was naturally eager to show that whatever the condition of Germany after the fighting she would not be able to regain a strategic ascendancy. As a result of the Paris Conference a special committee, under the chairmanship of that inveterate free-trader, Lord Balfour of Burleigh, was asked to produce an action report. The most important of its recommendations were:

> The producers of this country are entitled to require from the Government that they should be protected in the home market

against dumping—and against the introduction of sweated goods. Those industries which . . . [are] . . . key or pivotal should be maintained in this country at all hazards and at any expense.

Dumping, the practice by which countries disposed of their surplus products by exporting them at artificially low prices, was always frowned upon by free-traders who regarded it as unfair competition. It was not, therefore, surprising that Balfour of Burleigh favoured the first of these proposals. But the second recommendation implied straight protection, if only of a limited kind. Apparently, the sacrifices of war included long-cherished political ideals.

The Imperial Conference met in 1917. In the prevailing mood of comradely affection that was part of the war fever it was natural that the delegates should talk of economic cooperation. But on a more practical level Britain was at last showing signs that she was prepared to adapt her trade policy to take account of the needs of the dominions.

But it was not until 1919 that preference was offered to the dominions and then only on items of food, drink and tobacco already liable to import taxes. One problem was that the country was ruled by a coalition which contained Liberal and Labour free-traders as well as Conservative tariff reformers. Another inhibiting factor was the idealism of President Wilson of the United States, who intended that the conclusion of the war should provide the opportunity to dismantle the artificial barriers between nations. Armaments and tariffs were highest on his list of undesirable restraints on international brotherhood. Wilson was listened to with respect while he spoke with the backing of what was now the most powerful country in the world, but when his colleagues at home renounced his principle in favour of an isolationist policy, the European countries soon reverted to full blooded nationalism.

In 1921 Parliament approved the Safeguarding of Industries Act. It was in two parts, the first dealing with key industries like scientific instruments and certain chemicals, on which a duty of $33\frac{1}{3}$ per cent was imposed, and the second relating to dumping. Subject to an enquiry the Board of Trade was given the power to extend the tariff to any imported product selling below the cost of production or, because of currency depreciation abroad, selling below the cost of profitable production in Britain. To some free-traders it seemed that the chief intention of the Government was to secure fair terms of trade—a respectable ambition, after all—but others realised that the Bill could turn out to be a dangerously effective measure for introducing backdoor protection. This is precisely what happened. By 1926 the number of classes of goods covered by the dumping clauses had increased from 39 to 6,358. Imperial preference was offered on all duties.

With the Safeguarding of Industries Act securely on the statute book, the Conservative leadership decided, for the time being, not to risk another attack on free trade sentiment. The coalition government, under Lloyd George, broke up in 1922 and the Conservative Party fought the subsequent election on a programme of tranquillity and stability. Bonar Law promised merely that he would call yet another conference of Empire prime ministers to consider the best way of promoting imperial trade and repeated Balfour's pledge that no change would be made in the fiscal system without a second appeal to the nation. The tariff reformers sadly missed the crusading spirit of Joe Chamberlain, but they had to admit that Bonar Law was a shrewd judge of the mood of the country. The Conservatives were elected with a majority of seventy-three over all other parties, and the Liberals, with their 117 seats, were for the first time eclipsed by the Labour Party which was represented by 138 members. There was little time for Bonar Law to enjoy his triumph. In May 1923 his doctor diagnosed an incurable cancer of the throat. He resigned on 19 May without knowing that he had less than six months to live. His successor was Stanley Baldwin, Chancellor of the Exchequer in Bonar Law's Ministry.

The new Prime Minister came from a wealthy commercial background and worked on the principle that what was good for the businessmen was good for the country. He was a protectionist by conviction and listened sympathetically to appeals for an extension of the tariff. Among those who had the strongest claim for special attention were the leaders of the infant industries like the motor car manufacturers who need all the help they could get to fight off their American competitors. They had enjoyed a measure of protection since the introduction of the McKenna duties in 1917 and this, they claimed, was partly the reason for the rapid growth of their industry. A higher tariff would lead to further expansion.

Representatives of the older industries added their voices to the chorus. The postwar boom had fizzled out and now there was talk of a general depression which they were in no condition to survive. The iron and steel industry was badly in need of capital to bring its equipment up to date, and the coal mines were so antiquated that mechanical extraction was still thought to be outside the scope of their resources. Now, to make matters worse, most other countries were maintaining high tariffs to cushion their economies against fluctuations in world trade.

Finally, the imperial prime ministers at the economic conference in London, contributed their advice. The constant theme of their deliberations was preference, and yet more preference, for Empire products. But their greatest ambition was to persuade Britain to tax non-Empire agricultural imports, so far excluded from all protective measures. There were hints that relations between the dominions and the mother country might change radically if this concession was granted.

Baldwin gave encouragement to the protectionists when he spoke at the Conservative Conference at Plymouth on 26 October. Unemployment, which had reached a total of one million, was his major theme:

> Now from what I have said I think you will realise that to me, at least, this unemployment problem is the most crucial problem of our country. I regard it as such. I can fight it. I am willing to fight it. I cannot fight it without weapons. I have for myself come to the conclusion that—owing to the conditions that exist today in the world, having regard to the economic environment, having regard to the situation of our country—if we go pottering along as we are we shall have grave unemployment with us to the end of time. And I have come to the conclusion myself that the only way of fighting this subject is by protecting the home market. I am not a clever man. I know nothing of political tactics, but I will say this: Having come to that conclusion myself, I felt the only honest and right thing as a leader of a democratic party was to tell them, at the first opportunity I had, what I thought, and submit it to their judgment.

His modest estimate of his own abilities was not at first taken seriously by his colleagues. But within a few weeks their generosity had evaporated and the only characteristic they could find to praise in Baldwin was his honest confession of mediocrity. Inspired by the reception to his speech at the Conference the Prime Minister decided to offer the public a chance of recording their approval by holding a general election. If was one of the worst tactical blunders of modern politics. The public was unimpressed by Baldwin's desire to involve them in fiscal decisions. It was little more than a year since the Conservatives had been given a mandate to rule and now they were demanding a confirmation of that decision. It all seemed a waste of time and few observers were surprised when the Government lost nearly ninety seats to the Labour and Liberal Parties. The final results were

Conservatives	258
Labour	191
Liberal	158
Others	5

The Opposition parties combined to defeat Baldwin in the House of Commons and he resigned in favour of Ramsay MacDonald who led a minority Labour administration.

Why did Baldwin sacrifice his majority? The simple answer is that he genuinely believed that the country's economic problems, including unemployment, could only be solved by protection, and was prevented from introducing legislation on his own initiative by Bonar Law's pledge not to expand the tariff system without the express aproval of the voters. But as one observer pointed out:

No sane person with the slightest experience of political conditions in the cities where free trade was still associated with cheap food would have dreamed of confronting them with an election on the fiscal issue without taking some little time to put the Protectionist case before them again. Nobody outside a lunatic asylum—or the Unionist Central Office—would have given the eliminated Liberals and Socialists so heaven sent an opportunity to combine against the government (**12**).

An alternative theory is that Baldwin believed Lloyd George was about to declare himself in favour of protection. By so doing, it was thought, the ex-Prime Minister hoped to compete for power by gaining the support of Austen Chamberlain and other tariff re- formers. In fact, Lloyd George did briefly consider such a plan, but even so Baldwin exaggerated the danger (**7, 50, 66**).

The election brought the protection versus free trade issue into the open for the first time since Balfour led the Conservatives. Like his predecessor, Baldwin discovered that to produce a policy that could unite the Party was no less difficult than to compose a manifesto that could unite the country. Despite his hasty decision to invite the opinion of the voters he retained sufficient caution to exempt the major agricultural imports from his proposed tariffs. This was done partly to avoid the Labour and Liberal accusation that protection would raise the price of food and partly to satisfy the scruples of the remaining Conservative free traders, led by Lord Derby, whose electoral strength was concentrated in the northern constituencies. The tariff reformers interpreted compromise as cowardice and assumed that Baldwin was a leader in the same mould as Bonar Law and Balfour, distinguished only by his lack of tactical judgment.

Baldwin's toughest opponent among the tariff reformers was not even an MP. He was Lord Beaverbrook, the owner of the *Daily Express*, which he used to popularise the ideal of the nineteenth-century empire loyalists—imperial free trade. Beaverbrook was the son of a Presbyterian minister who preached in New Brunswick, Canada. His first business venture was a bowling alley in Calgary; by the time he was thirty his gift for commercial organisation had made him a millionaire. His ambition now was to enter politics and promote his concept of empire unity. He moved to London and joined forces with Bonar Law, another Canadian who sympathised with his aims. It was chiefly to promote Bonar Law that Beaverbrook bought the *Daily Express*, an almost bankrupt journal for which he paid a mere £17,500. He joined the power elite when Lloyd George became Prime Minister and remained close to the centre of government after Bonar Law took up residence in Downing Street. Along the way he acquired a peerage.

His influence declined with the succession of Baldwin, a politician he disliked and mistrusted. He advised against an election in 1923, and, while supporting the Conservatives throughout the campaign, made no secret of his disgust with Baldwin's compromise policy on protection. While the Labour Party discovered the problems of governing without a parliamentary majority, Beaverbrook played with the idea of founding a centre party with an economic policy based on imperial preference. He was supported by Lord Rothermere, owner of the *Daily Mail*. Their antipathy to Baldwin grew to such an intensity that the Conservative leader felt bound to retaliate. 'I am attacked by the Trust Press, by Lord Beaverbrook and Lord Rothermere. For myself I do not mind. I care not what they say or think. They are both men I would not have in my house. I do not respect them. Who are they . . .?' (**50**).

Such harsh comments were not at all suited to the public image of a mild-mannered country gentleman that he liked to project, and he later repudiated the statement, claiming that a newspaper reporter had misinterpreted his views. But almost certainly the reporter had done his job only too well.

Beaverbrook's campaign for imperial preference was entirely ineffectual while the Labour Party held office. The Chancellor of the Exchequer was Philip Snowden, a serious-minded Yorkshire-man whose pursuit of Socialist principles was tempered by a strong regard for orthodox finance (**23**). With his first budget he repealed the McKenna duties and refused to give another lease of life to those tariffs imposed to counteract the effect of depreciation in foreign currencies. Consequently the scope of imperial preference was severely reduced. The free-traders had won back nearly all the ground they had lost since the war. But there was little time for them to enjoy their revival. After less than a year in power the Labour Government was defeated on a motion of censure and MacDonald decided on a dissolution. The election was held in late October 1924.

Free trade was not a major issue of the campaign. The Labour manifesto did not mention tariffs and even the Liberals in their programme devoted only a short paragraph to the topic.

Baldwin led his party back to power with a majority of more than 200 over his Labour and Liberal opponents. Protectionism was in fashion again. The McKenna duties were rehabilitated and the Safeguarding procedure was extended to take in industries whose foreign competitors benefited from 'depreciation of currency operating so as to create an export bounty . . . subsidies, bounties and other artificial advantages . . . and inferior conditions of employ-ment of labour'. In an attempt to placate the dominions and the tariff reformers, who complained that a successful scheme of imperial preference depended on food taxes, Baldwin set up an Imperial Economic Committee whose members were given the responsibility of discovering ways and means of improving the sale of Empire foods in Britain.

During this period economists of all industrial countries shared a fear that tariff wars were getting out of hand and there were attempts to secure international agreements on trade restrictions. At a conference in Geneva in 1927 American and European delegates recommended a tariff armistice and during the next few months import duties were held at their existing level or even, in a few cases, reduced. At home Beaverbrook and the other extreme protectionists tempered their criticism of the now cautious Baldwin, while the international mood was against them and while domestic crises, like the General Strike of 1926, occupied the attention of the voters (**7**).

Then came the slump. It was born on the American Stock Exchange in October 1929. An exceptional boom in industrial investment had raised the value of shares to an unprecedented level. But towards the end of the year a number of speculators, working on the principle of what goes up must come down, thought it was about time they disposed of their shares while there was still a chance of maximising their capital gains. Once started, this sort of movement was difficult to contain. On 18 October the market was disappointing. The following day, there was a wave of selling. Within a week American commerce was ruled by panic.

In these circumstances, international trade was bound to suffer. The decline in foreign lending resulted in a drop in industrial production and national purchasing power. Primary producers discovered there was a lower demand for their exports and so raised tariffs to exclude imports for which they could not afford to pay. This made the situation worse for industrial exporters, who then raised their import duties in an effort to achieve a balance of trade. The repercussions of the tariff war might not have been so serious had the trading nations accepted the need to lower the barriers once production started to increase again. But despite the various conferences, customs agreements were negotiated on a narrow and unambitious level like the Oslo convention of 1930 between Norway, Sweden, Finland, Denmark, Holland and Belgium and the Ottawa agreement of 1932 between Britain and the Dominions (**11, 46**).

Shortly before the financial crisis hit Britain there was a general election, in which Labour won 287 seats against the Conservatives 260. The Liberals trailed behind with 59 seats, but they held the balance of power and decided to give their support to the largest single party. For the second time MacDonald formed a minority government. The early warning signs of the slump were reflected in the growing number of unemployed but, for the time being, the new administration was able to coast along without having to take drastic economic decisions. Meanwhile, the *enfant terrible* of the Conservative Party, Lord Beaverbrook, took upon himself the job of reminding Baldwin that Empire Free Trade was still a lively policy. A ten-week campaign in the *Daily Express* to raise support attracted a favourable response from 250,000 readers and the leader of the Opposition was sufficiently impressed to congratulate Beaverbrook on reviving the Empire theme. But he took a less charitable view of Lord Rothermere's 'Baldwin must go' campaign and his efforts to promote Beaverbrook as his only possible successor.

Relations between the parliamentary leadership and the press lords deteriorated still further when, in February 1930, they announced the formation of a United Empire Party, and threatened to 'contest half the seats in the country' at the next election [**docs. 15, 16**].

Beaverbrook made a tactical error by allying himself with the owner of the *Mail* and the *Sunday Pictorial*, even though these journals doubled his publicity resources. Francis Williams has described Lord Rothermere with brutal accuracy as 'a man almost wholly without political sophistication or even common judgment'. Under the banner of Empire Free Trade he paraded a troop of hobby horses, including a diplomatic break with Russia and an end to progress towards self-rule in India.

The crusade scored an early triumph when Vice-Admiral Taylor, a United Empire Party candidate, was elected in a by-election in Paddington. At East Islington, Brigadier General Critchley was not quite so lucky but he gained stronger support than the official Conservative candidate who was pushed into third place. The seat was won by a Socialist on a split vote. 'If the Conservative Party does not adopt Empire Free Trade,' said Beaverbrook, 'it is my purpose to break up the Party.' Even if it was a typically wild claim, to many Conservatives it seemed just possible that he might achieve the second of the alternatives. But they overestimated the power of the mass circulation dailies.

To the majority of readers the propaganda on the front pages had no greater significance than the racing results on the back. Baldwin, who was under pressure to make concession to the leaders of the Empire Crusade, succeeded in proving the point when Rothermere demanded, in return for electoral support in his newspapers, advance information as to 'the names of at least eight or ten of his most prominent colleagues in the next Ministry'. Public sympathy was on Baldwin's side when he replied: 'A more preposterous and insolent demand was never made on the leader of any political party. I repudiate it with contempt, and I will fight that attempt at domination to the end.'

He followed up this attack with one of the most famous speeches of any British party leader. At the Queen's Hall on 18 March 1931 when he spoke in support of Duff Cooper, the official Conservative candidate in the Westminster by-election, he told his audience:

> The papers conducted by Lord Rothermere and Lord Beaverbrook are not newspapers in the ordinary acceptance of the term. They are engines of propaganda for the constantly changing policies, desires, personal wishes, personal likes and dislikes of two men. What are their methods? Their methods are direct falsehood, misrepresentation, half-truths, the alteration of the speaker's meaning by pulling sentences apart from the context, suppression and editorial criticism of speeches which are not reported in the paper. What the proprietorship of these papers is aiming at is power, but power without responsibility—the prerogative of the harlot through the ages (**50, 66**).

The speech achieved all that Baldwin could have hoped. Duff Cooper defeated the Empire Free Trade candidate by a comfortable majority and much of the criticism of Baldwin as a Party leader was silenced. Thoroughly deflated, the press lords toned down their Empire Crusade and concentrated their energy on fighting each other for more readers for their publications. By 1933 Beaverbrook had the consolation of knowing that his was one of the largest newspaper circulations in the world. But political power eluded him.

Meanwhile the slump was exhausting the energy of the British people and their government. In 1930 there was a budget deficit of £14½ million with the prospect of lower tax revenues and increased expenditure on social assistance caused by unemployment and the run down of industry. The Chancellor of the Exchequer was Philip Snowden, a lifelong free-trader who was prepared to consider almost any remedy except the raising of the tariff barrier. His obstinacy brought him into conflict with the protectionists on the Conservative front bench, whom he accused of 'lying propaganda' when they attempted to argue that depressed industries might benefit from controls on cheap imports.

> The party opposite [he said, shortly before announcing his Budget for 1930] can put down fifty votes of censure between now and April 14th. They can put down a thousand questions on the Order Paper. The only answer they will get will be the answer which was given by the father of the Right Honourable Gentleman, the Member for Edgbaston [Neville Chamberlain]—the father of the modern protectionist movement—the only answer they will get are his words: 'What I have said, I have said' (**23**).

When 14 April came round, Snowden increased income tax, surtax and death duties, but lowered import duties on certain types of vehicles. But the Government still did not have the resources to cover its expenditure and with unemployment climbing past the two million mark, Snowden was soon borrowing £1 million a week to meet the excessive demands on the social insurance funds. In his next budget he introduced further increases in taxation without realising that by taking money out of the economy he was reducing spending power and imposing additional strain on industry and commerce. The Opposition produced their policy: tariffs and lower state expenditure, including cuts in the unemployment benefits, which would have had much the same general effect as Snowden's measures. Only a few lonely voices from the Liberal benches urged the Government to forget the budget deficit and pump money into the economy and solve the problem of unemployment by organising public works—road building, housing, afforestation—on a massive scale.

In May, following the run on the Austrian and German banks, the reserves of the Bank of England fell sharply as depositors withdrew gold. Demands for Government economies grew louder and more hysterical as politicians argued that a period of austerity would help restore confidence in sterling. Support for tariffs was also strengthened as importers, short of customers, dumped greater quantities of low priced products on the British market. Even the Liberals formed a protection group consisting of about one-third of the Party, and a majority of the members of the Government were sympathetic to the idea of a ten per cent revenue tariff.

Given a choice, Snowden naturally opted for economies and stood out for a 10 per cent cut in unemployment benefit as recommended by the May Committee, appointed by the Government. MacDonald refused to drop Snowden and give a lead to the protectionists, but the Cabinet could not reconcile their socialist principles with direct action against the unemployed. On 23 August, the Prime Minister had a meeting with the King, Baldwin and Sir Herbert Samuel, who represented the Liberals. That night the Labour Government resigned and MacDonald formed a national all party government. Snowden remained Chancellor but there were only three other Socialists—including MacDonald—in the Cabinet. There was a promise of an early appeal to the voters once Parliament had approved the economy measures (**61**).

In the election campaign that followed, one of the most confused in the history of British politics, the Conservatives emerged as victors. They dominated the new National Government with 471 seats while their Labour allies returned 13 members and the Liberals 35. Overall Labour representation was cut from 288 to 52. In the reshuffling of ministries, Snowden, now in poor health, was promoted to the peerage and given the job of Lord Privy Seal. Ironically, Neville Chamberlain became Chancellor at a time when a major part of his father's programme was about to be implemented. MacDonald was still Prime Minister, but it was Baldwin, as Lord President of the Council, who made the running on almost every aspect of policy.

'The Government', he said, 'must . . . be free to consider every proposal likely to help, such as tariffs, expansion of exports and contraction of imports, commercial treaties and mutually economic arrangements with the Dominions.' He made sure that the first important item of legislation was an Abnormal Importations Bill which empowered the Board of Trade to impose duties of up to 100 per cent. It was supposed to be a temporary measure, as was the Horticultural Products (Emergency Provisions) Bill which enabled 100 per cent duties to be placed on fruit and vegetables. But in early 1932 Parliament approved the Import Duties Bill which gave the seal of permanence to a general tariff of 10 per cent *ad valorem*. Additional duties could be imposed on the recommendation of an Import Duties Advisory Committee. Snowden and some of the Liberals threatened to resign, but decided to stay in the Government when they were allowed the unusual freedom of opposing their ministerial colleagues in open parliamentary debate.

Soon afterwards Baldwin and Chamberlain represented Britain

at an Imperial Economic Conference in Ottawa. The dominions recognised the strength of their bargaining position and though preferential agreements were signed—on condition they should remain in force for at least five years—the ideal of imperial unity was as remote as ever. It was too much for Snowden, who sent in his resignation, informing the Prime Minister that he could not 'acquiesce, even passively, in such a policy as national humiliation and bondage'. Several Liberal free-traders followed his example. It was the final defeat of free trade, but there was none of the excitement or hope of great economic victories that Joe Chamberlain or even Beaverbrook had anticipated. Protection was born of a crisis and its ascendancy was guaranteed because the British economy remained and still remains in a precarious state of imbalance.

Part Three

AFTERMATH

10 Towards European Unity

The second great war with Germany finally robbed Britain of her status as a world power. Looking back to the late 1940s it is easy enough to note the signs of an empire in decline. Industries that had been geared to supplying the military were in drastic need of new equipment and reorganisation. But capital and skilled labour were in short supply and there was no guarantee that the export markets neglected during the emergency could be held against American competition. Financing the war effort had resulted in a severe drop in the value of Britain's foreign investments and there were vast loans to be paid off to the United States. In comparison with the dominions, with their tremendous potential for economic growth, Britain was an old and tired country. Even those territories remaining under her direct rule campaigned energetically and successfully for the right to determine their own political future. India, 'the brightest jewel in the Empire', gained her independence in 1947, and that was only the beginning. For Britain the opportunities for playing grand international politics were almost exhausted.

At the time, however, most people did not judge the prospects quite so pessimistically. After all, Britain was on the winning side of a war that inflicted even worse damage on the economies of her European neighbours. She had a special relationship with the United States that enabled her to share the secrets of the latest military technology and if the Empire did seem to be wobbling dangerously, there was still a chance that the Commonwealth could shape itself into a major power bloc. Those politicians who were worried about Britain's future place in the world hierarchy were at least convinced that their country was in every way superior to Germany, the recent enemy, and France, the ally, whose second-hand victory was achieved at the expense of Anglo-American forces. The last thing they wanted was to get themselves entangled in European politics, except for reasons of national security. When imaginative leaders on the Continent made the first tentative moves towards European unity, Britain was unwilling to take part in an experiment that appeared so obviously to involve more trouble than it was worth.

Lord Gladwyn has pointed out that the idea of linking the European states in some sort of federal organisation can be traced to the late seventeenth century when William Penn, the founder of Pennsylvania, published his *Essay on the Present and Future Peace of Europe by the Establishment of a European Diet, Parliament and State* (**32**). In this century the first serious initiative was taken by the French Foreign Minister, Briand, when he addressed the League of Nations in 1929:

> I think that among peoples who are geographically grouped together like the peoples of Europe there must exist a sort of federal link. . . . It is this link which I wish to endeavour to establish. Evidently the association will act mainly in the economic sphere. That is the most pressing question. But I am sure also that from a political point of view, and from a social point of view the federal link, without infringing the sovereignty of any of the nations which might take part in such an association, could be beneficial.

Britain reacted coldly even to this cautious proposal.

After the second world war circumstances demanded cooperation on the lines indicated by Briand. Industrial and commercial reconstruction, financed largely by American aid, could be successful only if it was planned on a continental scale. The Organisation for European Economic Cooperation was set up with a membership consisting of most of the non-communist countries of Europe. Its job was to co-ordinate economic policies, give technical assistance to industry and agriculture, sponsor research and allocate new materials in short supply. Even some trade barriers were lowered, though the idea of a customs union was firmly rejected by Britain. This did not deter Belgium, the Netherlands and Luxembourg from adopting the plan for their own limited area.

Britain used the same blocking tactics against proposals to establish a European army. As an alternative, she helped to create the North Atlantic Treaty Organisation, which relied on the United States to deter Russia from further encroachment in the West. The Council of Europe, founded on the parliamentary principle and aiming 'to achieve a greater unity between its members for the purpose of safeguarding and realising the ideals and principles which are their common heritage, and facilitating their economic and social progress', was reduced to an advisory body chiefly by Britain's refusal to contemplate giving up any part of her sovereignty. Finally, the European Coal and Steel Community, the brainchild of Robert Schuman, French foreign minister, was repudiated by Britain. Schuman's idea was to reorganise these vital industries into a single group so as to achieve the economies of a large-scale production while avoiding the wasteful competitions caused by national rivalries. The scheme was a great success (**32, 45**).

This brief account of the progress towards European unity weights the scales rather heavily against Britain and it is only fair to point out that occasionally she had good reasons for her obstructive attitude. The European Army, for instance, was a good idea in theory but it is doubtful if adequate defence was possible in those early days of recovery without the assistance of the United States. In any case, Britain was not the only obstacle in the way of an integrated continental force. When the members of the Coal and Steel Community decided to establish a European Defence Community it was the French parliament that wrecked the plan.

But it was clear that Britain was too preoccupied with Commonwealth matters, her relationship with the United States and her power of independent action, to raise much enthusiasm for the European idea. Conservative and Labour politicians were sure that the memory of two world wars would slow up the unifying process however much energy was put into it and it came as a surprise when in March 1957, after two years' negotiations, France, Germany, Italy, Belgium, Holland and Luxembourg signed the Treaty of Rome, which laid down terms for the European Economic Community, or, as it was soon known, the Common Market. Among the important conditions agreed by the member states were the gradual reduction of internal barriers to trade, the setting up of a common external tariff and the abolition of restrictions on the movement of people, capital and goods within the Community.

Two years later seven of the European countries outside the Common Market—Austria, Denmark, Norway, Portugal, Sweden, Switzerland and Britain—formed the European Free Trade Association. It was seen as a defensive measure and no-one imagined that EFTA with a total population of nearly 100 million could match the potential of the Common Market with its superior economic resources and a population of 182 million. Observers forecast

105

that before long the two organisations would emerge. There was strong pressure on Britain to make the first move. Five of the six members of the Community were willing to support her application. The exception was France, whose ageing but energetic President, Charles de Gaulle, wanted the leadership of Europe for himself and his country. Political competition from a relatively powerful offshore island was something he could very well do without. He argued that Britain was not ready to join the Common Market, that her people were either opposed to European unity or half-hearted in their attachment to the concept [**docs 17, 18**].

In one sense he was right. The arch anti-European was Lord Beaverbrook, whose newspapers indulged in hysterical denunciations of the Community. 'The so-called United States of Europe has no attraction for the British people', claimed a leader writer in the *Daily Express*. 'The nation that resisted Napoleon and Hitler is not prepared to submit to Professor Hollstein, chief of the Common Market. Yet far stronger . . . is the conviction of the people: that to join Europe and sacrifice the Empire would be to betray the whole life and purpose of the British nation.'

Lord Beaverbrook had some excuse for his extravagant sentiments. His ideas for imperial free trade, the same ideas Joe Chamberlain had advocated in the later years of the nineteenth century, were, according to the politicians and economists, the product of starry-eyed idealism. Yet apparently, in a European context, free trade and unity were not only acceptable but enthusiastically acclaimed by most of the experts. No wonder Beaverbrook asked 'Where did we go wrong?' The answer, of course, was that the European nations, unlike the countries of the Empire and Commonwealth, were each in roughly the same stage of economic development with the added advantage of belonging to a recognisable geographical unit.

But reasons for failure of Empire free trade and the success of the European Community were not sufficient to persuade the anti-Marketeers to abandon their opposition to British entry. They argued that the mutual loyalties of the Commonwealth and the benefits of imperial preference were not worth sacrificing for the sake of the European export market.

Those who favoured a British application to join the Community pointed out that members of the Commonwealth were not quite so preoccupied with their historic links with the mother country. To Britain, the value of imperial preference had declined over the years.

The Commonwealth received 60 per cent of its capital outside the British money market and imports from and exports to Britain were falling. When Australia had faced a balance of payments problem, she had not hesitated to impose a special tariff that virtually excluded British cars. Most other Commonwealth countries were equally unsentimental when it came to important economic decisions.

The exception was New Zealand. Over half of all her exports were sent to Britain and this included as much as 90 per cent of her exports of butter, cheese and lamb. A European tariff raised against her might have wrecked her economy. But there seemed no reason why special provisions could not be negotiated to prevent any serious harm to New Zealand. Encouraged by the success of the Community, the prospect of solving domestic economic problems by gaining entry to one of the richest export markets in the world, and the shift in public opinion that became evident when people realised that the country would not be swamped by cheap European labour or burdened by massive increases in food prices, the Conservative government, in August 1961, made formal application to join the Six.

The rest of the story is too well documented to repeat in detail. Negotiations were blocked by France and talks were broken off in January 1963. A Labour government tried again in 1967 only to achieve the same depressing result (**36**). Now, in 1970, following the retirement of President de Gaulle, preparations are being made for another application. As Dean Acheson, one of America's most respected politicians, said in 1962: 'Great Britain has lost an Empire and has not yet found a role.' She is still looking.

During the last twenty years Britain has made some contribution to the reduction of world tariffs. She has joined, with more than forty other countries, the General Agreement on Tariffs and Trade and negotiated small but useful limits on import restrictions. She has taken part in the Kennedy Round, an American inspired attempt to accelerate tariff cuts under GATT and she has played the chief role in founding EFTA. But her attempts to increase her political and economic authority by joining a European Common Market have so far met with the same frustrating failures as her efforts to create an Imperial Common Market. The alternative prospects for the future are economic isolationism with the probability of capturing a declining share of world trade, a successful application to enter Europe or an Atlantic free trade agreement (**38**). Is it possible that Britain's future is not with the dominions or Europe, but with the United States, the very first of the colonies to break away from the Empire?

Part Four

DOCUMENTS

The League

The leaders of the Anti-Corn Law League fought a political battle on two fronts. They were opposed on one side by the landowners who were convinced that a fall in the price of bread would lead to their economic destruction. At the other end of the social scale, the Chartists, who claimed to represent working-class opinion, believed that the campaign for cheaper bread was really an attempt by employers to find an excuse for cutting wages.

Virulent attacks on The League were published in the Chartist newspaper, The Northern Star.

THE LEAGUE

Who are that blustering, canting crew,
Who keep the cheap loaf in our view,
And would from us more profit screw?
           The League.

Who cry 'Repeal the curs'd Corn Law,'
And would their workmen feed with straw,
That they may filthy lucre paw?
           The League.

Who wish to gull the working man,
And burk the Charter, if they can,
With their self-aggrandising plan?
           The League.

Who deal in sophistry and cant—
Of common sense evince the want—
And strive the Charter to supplant?
           The League.

Who meet defeat at every turn,
From the Chartists, strong and stern,
Yet from it wisdom will not learn?
                    The League.

Who have receiv'd their final fall,
This afternoon, on our Cloth Hall
And there not one more meeting call?
                    The League.

William Ryder, *The Northern Star*, 3 April 1841.

The Corn Laws and Emigration

The Chartists argued that the Corn Laws were only an indirect cause of the working man's poverty. The root problem was the greediness of the landowners who demanded high rents from their tenant farmers.

THE CORN LAWS AND EMIGRATION

Because our lords have taxed the staff of life,
The working man, his children, and his wife
All slave together, yet they must not eat—
Toil gives an appetite, but brings no meat!
The price of bread by law is kept so high,
That what we earn suffices not to buy.
But, why is this? What makes our bread so dear?
Far cheaper 'tis abroad than it is here!
Yes, but a tax is laid on forein grain,
To make our home-grown corn its price maintain;
And half-fed men may toil, and starve, and die,
That idle lords may lift their heads on high.
We might buy cheap, but landlords want great rents,
To spend in keeping grand establishments.
Their feast, their fancies, jewels, balls and plays,
The poor man's nakedness and hunger pays.
The tenant says, if corn comes duty free,
'Twill bring down prices here, and ruin me:
Taxes and rents in England are so high,
I cannot sell so cheap as you could buy.
Pensions, and perquisites, all other prices
Must come down too, save luxuries and vices.
The honest husbandman must emigrate,
And leave poor peasants to increase the rate,
Unless our lords consent to live on less,
And pride succumb to humble happiness!

John Watkins, *The Northern Star*, 1 January 1842.

113

The Corn Laws and Poverty

The League's opposition to the Corn Laws was based on the principles of free trade. Abolish the restrictions on international commerce, said Cobden and Bright, and the consequent industrial expansion would bring an end to poverty.

Our opponents tell us that our object in bringing about the repeal of the Corn Laws, is, by reducing the price of corn, to lower the rate of their wages. I can only answer upon this point for the manufacturing districts; but, as far as they are concerned, I state it most emphatically as a truth, that, for the last twenty years, whenever corn has been cheap wages have been high in Lancashire; and, on the other hand, when bread has been dear wages have been greatly reduced. . . .

Now, let me be fully understood as to what Free Traders really do want. We do not want cheap corn merely in order that we may have low money prices. What we desire is plenty of corn, and we are utterly careless what its price is, provided we obtain it at the natural price. All we ask is this, that corn shall follow the same law which the monopolists in food admit that labour must follow that 'it shall find its natural level in the markets of the world'. . . .

To pay for that corn, more manufacturers would be required from this country; this would lead to an increased demand for labour in the manufacturing districts, which would necessarily be attended with a rise of wages, in order that the goods might be made for the purpose of exchanging for the corn brought from abroad. . . . I observe there are narrow-minded men in the agricultural districts, telling us, 'Oh, if you allow Free Trade, and bring in a quarter of corn from abroad, it is quite clear that you will sell one quarter less in England'. . . . What! I would ask, if you set more people to work at better wages— if you can clear your streets of those spectres which are now haunting your thoroughfares begging their daily bread—if you can depopulate your workhouses and clear off the two million of paupers which now exist in the land, and put them to work at productive industry—do you not think that they would consume some of the wheat as well as you; and may not they be, as we are now, consumers of wheaten bread by millions, instead of existing on their present miserable dietary?

Richard Cobden, *Speeches* (1870), i, 118–33.

Disraeli attacks Peel

*During the debate on the abolition of the Corn Laws, Disraeli made
one of the most brilliant speeches of his career, in which he labelled
Peel as a betrayer of his Party and a traitor to those who had made him
leader. His choice of analogy to illustrate his theme was calculated to
cause the Prime Minister the maximum pain and embarrassment.*

Sir, there is a difficulty in finding a parallel to the position
of the right hon. gentleman in any part of history. The only
parallel which I can find is an incident in the late war in the
Levant, which was terminated by the policy of the noble lord
opposite. I remember when that great struggle was taking
place, when the existence of the Turkish Empire was at stake,
the late Sultan, a man of great energy and fertile in resources,
was determined to fit out an immense fleet to maintain his
empire. Accordingly a vast armament was collected. The crews
were picked men, the officers were the ablest that could be
found, and both officers and men were rewarded before they
fought. There was never an armament which left the Dardan-
elles similarly appointed since the days of Solyman the Great.
The Sultan personally witnessed the departure of the fleet; all
the muftis prayed for the expedition, as all the muftis here
prayed for the success of the last general election. Away went
the fleet, but what was the Sultan's consternation when the
Lord High Admiral steered at once into the enemy's port.
Now, sir, the Lord High Admiral on that occasion was very
much misrepresented. He, too, was called a traitor, and he, too,
vindicated himself. 'True it is,' said he, 'I did place myself
at the head of this great armada; true it is that my sovereign
embraced me; true it is that all the muftis in the Empire offered
up prayers for the expedition; but I have an objection to war.
I see no use in prolonging the struggle, and the only reason I

had for accepting the command was that I might terminate the contest by betraying my master.'

Hansard, 3rd series, 83, 111–23, reports the speech in full.

John Bright and federation

The concept of imperialism was anathema to the traditional free traders who regarded colonial expansion at best as an expensive luxury and at worst as an attempt by one country to dominate a section of international commerce. Not surprisingly, John Bright was among those who opposed federation, and in particular, any attempt to use tariff agreements to establish a closer link between Britain and her Empire.

I think nothing can be more useless and impracticable than any attempt to bring colonial members into the English Parliament. We do not legislate for the colonies; they cannot legislate for us. Their numbers would be as nothing in our Parliament. They could be of no use to us, and they would be incapable of any good for the colonies from which they came. The project, in my view, is absurd and does not need any discussion.

These ideas of 'federation' between England and her colonies are equally visionary and valueless. What is intended by 'federation' I do not know. But surely trade is meant and surely free trade—not a Canadian or a Victorian tariff. We now give the colonies everything—we buy almost all they have to sell and levy no duty on their exports, none for protection. What can we do more? If they want a nearer alliance with us, they can give up their tariffs; we can give them nothing more.

Our people are all friends of the colonies, but common sense in dealing with our brethren in distant regions is worth far more than the feeble sentiment which some dreamers seem anxious to encourage.

Letter from John Bright to D. Fraser Lumsden (Melbourne), *The Times*, 26 October 1897.

Made in Germany

In January 1896 the 'New Review' published the first of six monthly articles by E. E. Williams under the heading 'Made in Germany'. The articles, which were later published in book form, found a wide readership and effectively destroyed any illusions of commercial superiority which might have remained in the hearts of British loyalists.

Take observations, Gentle Reader, in your own surroundings. . . . You will find that the material of some of your own clothes was probably woven in Germany. Still more probable is it that some of your wife's garments are German importations; while it is practically beyond a doubt that the magnificent mantles and jackets wherein her maids array themselves on the Sundays out are German-made and German-sold, for only so could they be done at the figure. Your governess's fiancé is a clerk in the City; but he was also made in Germany; nay, the material of your favourite (Patriotic) newspaper had the same birthplace as like as not. Roam the house over, and the fateful mark will greet you at every turn, from the piano in your drawing-room to the mug on your kitchen dresser, blazoned though it be with the legend, 'A Present from Margate'. Descend to your domestic depths, and you shall find your very drain-pipes German made. You pick out of the grate the paper wrappings from a book consignment, and they also are 'Made in Germany'. You stuff them into the fire, and reflect that the poker in your hand was forged in Germany . . . And so the story goes on until, . . . you drop off to sleep only to dream that St Peter, (with a duly stamped halo round his head and a bunch of keys from the Rhineland), has refused you admission into Paradise, because you bear not the mark of the Beast upon your forehead, and are not made in Germany.

E. E. Williams, *Made in Germany*, p. 10.

British trade methods

The appearance of a Government report criticising British trade methods provided 'The Times' with an opportunity to publish a stinging attack on exporters who refused to modernise their selling techniques.

British merchants have so far failed to adapt themselves to the transition going on all around them from monopoly to competition. It pains and surprises them to find that the goods they offer, though acknowledged to be superior are not preferred by the benighted foreign purchaser to the inferior goods offered by their upstart rivals. The benighted purchaser humbly suggests that the article they offer is not exactly to his taste. 'Take it or leave it,' they haughtily answer, in the true spirit of the monopolist; 'if you don't know a good British article when you see it, that's your lookout,' and the benighted foreigner too often suits the action to the word—and leaves it. The British merchant produces and scatters . . . the most beautifully printed and illustrated catalogues of his goods. But they are printed in a language which the foreigner does not understand, the weights and measures are given in denominations he has never heard of, the prices are quoted in a currency which he cannot readily convert to his own, and they rarely include the cost of freight, duty, and delivery to his own port or railway station. The British merchant, by comparison with his German rival, employs very few commercial travellers abroad, and those he does employ too often speak no language but their own. He has his own method of packing, which is adopted to suit his own convenience not that of his customer, and is in many cases a serious impediment to the sale of his wares. He despises small orders, rarely risking a sprat to catch a whale and he is stiff and uncompromising in the matter of granting credit facilities adapted to the habits of business in vogue with his foreign customers.

The Times, Leader, 14 November 1898. Inspired by the Board of Trade reports on trade in South America and the Parliamentary Paper 'Opinion of Her Majesty's Diplomatic and Consular Officers on British Trade Methods'.

Joseph Chamberlain's Tariff Reform Speech at Birmingham, 15 May 1903

. . . It seems to me not at all an impossible assumption that before the end of this present century we may find our fellow-subjects beyond the seas as numerous as we are at home. I want you to look forward. I want you to consider the infinite importance of this not only to yourselves but to your descendants. Now is the time when you can exert influence. Do you wish that if these ten millions become forty millions they shall still be closely, intimately, affectionately, united to you, or do you contemplate the possibility of their being separated, going off each in his own direction, under a separate flag? Think what it means to your power and influence as a country; think what it means to your position among the nations of the world; think what it means to your trade and commerce—I put that last. The influence of the Empire is the thing I think most about, and that influence, I believe, will always be used for the peace and civilisation of the world.

But the question of trade and commerce is one of the greatest importance. Unless that is satisfactorily settled, I for one do not believe in a continued union of the Empire. I hear it stated again and again by what I believe to be the representatives of a small minority of the people of this country, those whom I describe, because I know no other words for them, as 'Little Englanders'—I hear it stated by them, what is a fact, that our trade with those countries is much less than our trade with foreign countries, and therefore it appears to be their opinion that we should do everything in our power to cultivate that trade with foreigners, and that we can safely disregard the trade with our children.

That is not my conclusion. My conclusion is exactly the opposite. To look into the future, I say that is the business of British tradesmen to do everything they can, even at some present sacrifice, to keep the trade of the Colonies with Great Britain, to increase the trade and to promote it, even if in doing so we lessen somewhat the trade with our foreign competitors. . . .

My policy, which I wish to make clear to you, is not to force our Colonies—that is hopeless, they are as independent as we are—but to meet everything they do. If they see a way of drawing the Empire together let us help them in that, even if they may not be prepared to join us in some other way from which we think the same result would be achieved. But let us be prepared to accept every indication on their part of this desire; let us show we appreciate it, and believe me, it will not be long before all will come into line, and the results which follow will be greater than, perhaps, it would be prudent now to anticipate.

What has Canada done for us?

Canada in 1898 freely and voluntarily of her own accord, as a recognition of her obligations to the Mother Country, as a recognition especially of the fact that we were the greatest of the free markets open to Canadian produce, gave us a preference on all dutiable goods of 25 per cent. In 1900 she increased that preference, also freely of her own accord, to $33\frac{1}{3}$ per cent. . . .

But the Ministers of Canada when they were over here last year made me a further definite offer. They said: 'We have done for you as much as we can do voluntarily and freely and without return. If you are willing to reciprocate in any way, we are prepared to reconsider our tariff with a view of seeing whether we cannot give you further reductions, especially in regard to those goods in which you come into competition with foreigners, and we will do this if you will meet us by giving us a drawback on the small tax of 1s per quarter which you have put on corn.' Well, that was the offer which we had to refuse. I must say that if I could treat matters of this kind solely in regard to my position as Secretary of State for the Colonies I should have said, 'That is a fair offer, that is a generous offer from your point of view, and it is an offer which we might ask our people to accept.' But speaking for the Government as a whole, not in the interests of the Colonies, I am obliged to say, that it is contrary to the established fiscal policy of this country, and that we hold ourselves bound to keep an open market for all the world even if they close their markets to us, and that therefore so long as that is the mandate of the British public, we are not in a position to offer any preference or favour whatever, even to our own children. . . .

In my mind that is putting us in a rather humiliating position. I do not like it at all. I know what will follow if we allow it to prevail. It is easy to predict the consequences. How do you think that in such circumstances we can approach our Colonies with appeals to aid us in promoting the union of the Empire, or ask them to bear a share of the common burdens. . . .

I leave the matter in your hands. I desire that a discussion on this subject [imperial preference] should be opened. The time has not yet come to settle it, but it seems to me that for good or for evil this is an issue much greater in its consequences than any of our local disputes.

Make a mistake in legislation. It can be corrected. Make a mistake in your Imperial policy. It is irretrievable. You have an opportunity; you will never have it again. I do not think myself that a general election is very near, but whether it is near or distant, I think our opponents may perhaps find that the issues which they propose to raise are not the issues on which we shall take the opinion of the country. If we raise an issue of this kind the answer will depend not on petty personal considerations, not on temporary interest, but on whether the people of this country really have it in their hearts to do all that is necessary, even if it occasionally goes against their own prejudices, to consolidate an Empire which can only be maintained by relations of interest as well as by relations of sentiment. And for my own part I believe in a British Empire, in an Empire which, though it should be its first duty to cultivate friendship with all the nations of the world, should yet, even if alone, be self-sustaining and self-sufficient, able to maintain itself against the competition of all its rivals.

The Times, 16 May 1903.

Intellectual repercussions

L. S. Amery, later one of Chamberlain's strongest supporters, describes in his autobiography the public reaction to the Birmingham speech.

In the few hours [after Chamberlain's speech of 15 May] England, and indeed the whole Empire, were in a ferment of indescribable excitement. In teaching his countrymen to think imperially Chamberlain had builded better than he knew. . . . In its protest against the intolerable tyranny of a meaningless economic formula, the speech kindled into instant flame all the embers of doubt and suspicion about the infallibility of Free Trade, which had been silently smouldering for years.

Like another Tetzel in his pragmatic defence of the preposterous, Ritchie had precipitated a great intellectual crisis. The Birmingham speech was a challenge to free thought as direct and provocative as the theses which Luther nailed to the church door at Wittemburg. Men who on 15 May would have resented being described as anything but Free Traders, found themselves within a few days hating Free Trade with all the intensity with which any Calvinist ever hated the Church of Rome. On the other hand, many who would have accepted a preferential reduction of the corn duties with indifference, or even satisfaction, suddenly shrank back in dismay from the terrifying vista now opening out to their sight. A complete remoulding, not only of British policy, but, harder still, of their intellectual outlook, and of their whole mental stock in-trade of familiar and comforting phrases and formulas—instinct bade them avert at all hazards such a disaster. Add to this intellectual ferment the fierce hunger of an Opposition long cheated of its hopes of office, and looking eagerly for some topic to close its own ranks and break up those of its opponents, the anxious shepherding of Government party managers only intent on preventing a dissolution, and the individual ambitions of rising politicians, and it becomes possible to form some conception of the confused struggle which now began—a struggle which coloured, even when it did not dominate, English politics for decades, and in the course of which the original object of Chamberlain's policy seemed at times to be almost forgotten by those who professed to be his followers. . . .

In my own case I had gone on the morning of 16 May to my room at *The Times* office in the usual way to work at my History [of the Boer War]. But my mind was on far wider horizons than the South African battlefields when in burst Leo Maxse. Seizing both my hands in his he waltzed me round the room as he poured forth a paean of jubilation at the thought that, at last, there was cause to work for in politics. The next few weeks were largely spent in a spate of discussion, persuading or converting all whom I met.

L. S. Amery, *My Political Life*, i, 236–40.

Balfour, Chamberlain and Protection

On 16 September 1903 Lord George Hamilton wrote to Lord Curzon, Viceroy of India, explaining that his resignation was inevitable because Balfour was apparently unwilling to repudiate Chamberlain.

As I anticipated we could come to no agreement at our Cabinet on Monday. The Balfour–Chamberlain alliance is an impossible combination for those who are opposed to Joe's protectionist and preferential ideas. Arthur differentiates, poses as a Free Trader, puts forward protectionist principles with limitations, which must disappear if the principles are carried. Chamberlain whilst ready to resign, openly states that he must adhere, whether in office or out of it, to the Preferential scheme, but he adds 'I am not Prime Minister and my colleagues are not necessarily bound by what I say.' But if the Prime Minister will not repudiate his theories we lesser men have no alternative but to go. A. J. cannot afford to part with Chamberlain just now, he may be right, so we mediocrities must go!

Hamilton Papers.

The Cabinet and food taxation

Devonshire wrote to the Prime Minister on 15 September 1903 suggesting that if duties on food were omitted from Government policy there would be no resignations.

Before sending you my final decision I should like to know if possible what it is that you propose to say about preferential treatment of the Colonies involving taxation of food. Though I understand you to doubt its practicability at the present time, I do not understand that you will say anything that will prevent Chamberlain from continuing his advocacy of it.

We are all I believe agreed that the time has come when the Cabinet must cease to speak with two voices, and therefore I do not think that any reservations on your part short of rejection of this part of the policy would make much difference in the situation, though I have reason to believe that a distinct repudiation of it would affect the views of other members of the Government, perhaps more than my own.

Balfour Papers.

Devonshire resigns from the Cabinet

Devonshire wrote to Balfour offering his resignation on the evening of 15 September 1903.

I need not tell you that I have given the most anxious thought to the discussion in yesterday's Cabinet and to the conversation which I had with you afterwards—nor is it necessary for me to say with what deep regret I find that I cannot come to any other conclusion than that which I have indicated in two or three recent letters to you as the probable one.

My conviction that I cannot with satisfaction to myself, or with any advantage to the Government remain a member of it after the declaration of policy which you intend to make at Sheffield is strengthened by what took place at the Cabinet yesterday.

Two members of the Cabinet only had written and circulated Minutes on the questions under discussion. Ritchie and Balfour of Burleigh. I have referred again to these Minutes, and I find that they consist mainly of criticisms on the procedure that has been adopted, of the expression of doubt as to the necessity of any new departure at all in our fiscal policy, and of objections to any plan of fiscal reform, which in the absence of any definite plan proposed by the reformers, it seemed possible to construct from the speeches of Mr Chamberlain. I do not find these Minutes a single criticism from which I dissent, or any argument with which in the absence of reply and repudiation, I disagree. But without any attempt to reply to these criticisms or objections, without any statement whatever on the part of the principal authors of the new departure, it was assumed that the writers had shown themselves to be irreconcilable, and that their resignation has become inevitable. I do not question the opinion expressed on all sides yesterday that this policy can only be successful if supported by men who

129

thoroughly believe in it, and I ask myself how it is possible that I who so largely share the views of these Ministers who are deemed to be irreconcilable, can under any conceivable circumstances be of any use to or add to the strength of the Government.

. . . a crisis similar to this one was imminent in the Summer, and was only averted by the invention of the formula of the Enquiry. I have done my best to persuade myself and to persuade others that a real Enquiry was being carried on, that Free Trade was on its trial, and that by the results of the Enquiry it would be judged. But I cannot admit that the collection of a mass of statistics without any attempt to enlighten ourselves or the country as to what they prove, or an abstract essay such as you intend to publish constitute the kind of Enquiry which I at least have been promising. I object therefore to the declaration which you propose to make at Sheffield that the time has arrived when it is necessary that a change, which I understand you will indicate as a considerable change, must be made in the fiscal policy of the country.

Balfour Papers.

Balfour and Chamberlain come to terms

Correspondence between Balfour and Chamberlain published in The
Times *on 14 February 1906 and known as the Valentine letters established a common policy on tariff reform.*

Balfour to Chamberlain
The controversy aroused by the Fiscal Question has produced,
not unnaturally, an impression which I have constantly com-
bated, that the practical differences between fiscal reformers
are much deeper than is in fact the case. The exchange of views
which has recently taken place between us leads me to hope
that this misconception may be removed, and with it much
friction which has proved injurious to the Party.

My own opinion, which I believe is shared by the great
majority of the Unionist Party may be briefly summarised as
follows:

I hold that Fiscal Reform is, and must remain, the first
constructive work of the Unionist Party.

That the objects of such reform are to secure more equal
terms of competition for British trade, and closer commercial
union with the Colonies.

That, while it is at present unnecessary to prescribe the
exact methods, by which these objects are to be attained, and
inexpedient to permit differences of opinion as to those methods
to divide the Party, though other means may be possible, the
establishment of a moderate general tariff on manufactured
goods, not imposed for the purpose of raising prices or giving
artificial protection against legitimate competition, and the
imposition of a small duty on foreign corn, are not in principle
objectionable, and should be adopted if shown to be necessary
for the attainment of the ends in view or for purposes of revenue.

131

Chamberlain's reply

I cordially welcome your letter of today, in which you have summarised the conclusions that we have reached during our recent discussion.

I entirely agree with your description of the objects which we both have in view, and gladly accept the policy which you indicate as the wise and desirable one for the Unionist Party to adopt.

In endeavouring to give effect to this policy and in defending all Unionist principles, any services that I can render will be entirely at your disposal.

Balfour and Party unity

J. S. Sandars, Balfour's private secretary, wrote formally to the Opposition leader in January 1907 explaining the fears of the tariff reformers and urging a more positive line on the tariff issue.

It is pointed out by the more ardent section [of the tariff reformers] that since your letter of 14 February last year, nothing has been said, no public speeches have been made by you in furtherance of this—the first constructive test of the Unionist Party. They do not argue that you wish to go back on your words; they do say that the policy of Fiscal Reform does not fill your heart and mind; they argue that in a case where you are really and profoundly moved, as in the matter of Education, you will fight, and fight hard, and spend the last ounce of your strength over it. And they contrast the matter in which you are interested with that which does not earn a speech, or part of a speech. . . . The rank and file clamour for some broad line of policy above and beyond resisting and denouncing a Government no matter how pernicious it may be. . . . They thoroughly appreciate your great services to the Party, your ripe experience, and the extraordinary skill you exhibit in leading the Party in Parliament. But they are not proof against the blandishments of those who promise that they can sweep the country with a fiscal policy that will be of enormous national benefit, and they cannot be made to see that their chance will come the sooner if only they will concentrate on the iniquities of the most vulnerable Government of modern times. If you do not speak on the fiscal question, then the malcontents will declare that their contention is well founded and that you are indifferent to the Tariff issue. . . . The bulk of the Party do not for a moment desire that you should commit yourself to details . . . but they do want a statement on broad lines touching Fiscal Reform in its relation to finance both Imperial and local; they would like a sympathetic reference to closer commercial union with the Colonies; they would like a point made of the fact that schemes of social reform cannot be accomplished without the elasticity of revenue which alone can be obtained from a wider basis of taxation. . . . A speech on these lines would, in Hood's [Sir Alexander Acland Hood, Chief Opposition Whip] opinion, pull the Party together. The point is—are you disposed to make it? It may in your judgement be unwise to make it. Be it so—but then, says Hood, we shall practically lose our army—very likely not all at once, but by degrees, until anarchy is succeeded by a new authority. . . .

I may observe that Hood has never mentioned to me the question of food taxation. *Personally* I consider the case as hopeless, so long as we advocate a policy which embraces it. In writing thus frankly to you even as the mouthpiece of others, I do not fail to see . . . the egregious folly of those who . . . wish to sacrifice a proportion of their strength by making themselves responsible for a constructive policy, which is just the target that their opponents want. But you have to take men as you find them, and if they will choose the path of difficulty it still behoves you—their leader—to guide them, doesn't it? How best to do it is the question.

Balfour's reply
Thanks much for your most lucid, interesting and excellent letters. As regards the one on the Party and Tariff Reform, I was well acquainted with almost all that it contains . . .

I rather propose telling the Party the 'truth in love' at Hull, and not waiting for the 15th, where however I could repeat the lesson if it were necessary. I shall of course have to touch on Tariff Reform, and say what I have so often said before, but what apparently our Tariff Reform friends are never tired of hearing. I am by no means sure that we shall not have to carry the war into the enemy's camp and make it quite clear that if the Party is to be destroyed—which can easily be done by either wing—the disloyal TRs have at least as much to lose as anybody else. But this is a policy only to be adopted in the last resort.

Blanche Dugdale, *Arthur James Balfour*, pp. 31–2.

Lord Beaverbrook's crusade

IMPORTANT SPEECH AT HASTINGS
CRITICISM OF CONSERVATIVE CENTRAL OFFICE
DODGING THE ISSUE
TRIBUTE TO LORD ROTHERMERE

The Empire Crusade swept victoriously into Hastings tonight before three great gatherings of nearly six thousand people.

The two halls of the White Rock Pavilion were jammed to the doors, and an overflow of more than a thousand people gathered outside to hear Lord Beaverbrook in the open air.

It was an evening of successive victories, with Senator Elliott, the leader of the Country Party in the Australian Senate helping to carry the cause of Empire Free Trade to a momentous triumph.

Lord Beaverbrook spoke to all three gatherings, and galvanised the crowds into a demonstration of tremendous enthusiasm. . . .

Lord Beaverbrook in his speech first paid tribute to those who had supported the Empire Crusade movement, though at first it had met with opposition and derision, especially from the existing political parties.

'But the vision of the people is wider than the vision of the politicians,' he said, 'and from small beginnings the movement has grown, until now the tide is running strongly in our favour.

'There is, however, one man to whom I would pay a special tribute for the invaluable support which he has given us throughout our whole campaign. That man is Lord Rothermere. . . .

'I must confess, however, that lately we have been disappointed with the attitude of the leaders of the Conservative Party. Although this is the party to which we look for our greatest measure of support, they show little zeal for the policy of Empire Free Trade.

'Their speeches are devoted largely to defending themselves against the imputation that the next election will be fought on the issue of food taxes.

'We are told that, if only we will show a little patience, the Conservative Party will embrace our policy in its entirety. They are to be given time, and then they will see the full light of day. But how can we go on waiting with 1,700,000 people on the unemployment registers? . . .'

Daily Express, 20 May 1930.

The North Norfolk By-election

It is the attitude of the Socialists which will largely determine the issue. Lord Beaverbrook reveals no secret when he declares that two hundred Socialist Members of Parliament support the principles of Empire Free Trade. In addition, the Economic Committee of the Trade Union Congress General Council have taken their stand on the same platform.

Mr MacDonald knows that he cannot lead his party in a general election with any hope of success against a united Conservative Party pledged to bring in Empire Free Trade. That is why he is brooding so heavily with eyes fixed on Mr Snowden, the unrepentant Free Importer, as if to say, 'Will no one rid me of this turbulent Chancellor?'

The Liberals, of course, are split from stem to stern. They have seen their own great Chancellor of the Exchequer, Mr McKenna, sign the death warrant of Cobdenism. They have seen their former Chief Whip, Mr McCurdy, and former Ministers, such as Lord Islington and Sir John Pratt, range themselves openly on the side of Empire Free Trade.

Mr Lloyd George alone remains cheerful for the present. He knows quite rightly that history will remember him when Cobdenism is forgotten.

Yet his cheerfulness is in the face of the fact that already a vast section of Liberal opinion throughout the country is solidly behind Lord Beaverbrook and Empire Free trade.

FOR AND AGAINST

Reduced to its simplest terms, the political situation resolves itself into this division of opinion:—

For Empire Free Trade	Against Empire Free Trade
Conservatives 90%	Conservatives 5%
Liberals 40%	Liberals 50%
Socialists 65%	Socialists 20%

Undecided: Conservatives 5%. Liberals 10%. Socialists 15%.

It is the recognition of this political balance sheet which is altering the whole trend of events. Both in Liberal and Socialist circles it is being urged that the Conservatives, by their hesitation and timidity, have lost any right to claim Empire Free Trade as their own, and that a free vote in the House of Commons would bring in Empire Free Trade as the law of the land by a large majority.

Current opinion is hardening to this measure, and it was being freely stated during the week-end that before the next dissolution the House would divide on the issue, with the Whips called off, Mr MacDonald and Mr Baldwin leading the majority into one lobby, and Mr Snowden and Mr Lloyd George gathering up the remainder of those who do not abstain.

In the meantime all eyes are turned on North Norfolk. The electors there have had the issue placed before them with a thoroughness which is almost unprecedented.

If North Norfolk, a Socialist constituency, returns Mr Cook as the Empire Free Trade candidate, it will be a decisive factor in determining the attitude of the Government towards the Imperial question.

If, on the other hand, Lady Noel-Buxton is returned as the anti-Empire Free Trade candidate (the platform on which she is fighting), it will encourage the Little Englanders under the misguided fanaticism of Mr Snowden to work for an immediate appeal to the electorate on old party lines and worn-out shibboleths.

That is why Lord Beaverbrook is straining every nerve to secure from North Norfolk something greater than a by-election victory—he is asking the farmers and farm-workers of North Norfolk for a mandate in favour of Empire Free Trade for the whole country.

Daily Express, 7 July 1930.

The by-election was won by Lady Noel-Buxton but Cook had his revenge in the 1931 election when he gained the seat for the Conservatives.

Britain is rejected by the Common Market

Britain was today formally refused entry into the European Economic Community. The Foreign Ministers of West Germany, Italy and the Benelux countries accepted the fact that the French Government was determined to veto the British application for membership.

Whatever may happen all over the world, there was bitter regret in Brussels. The Dutch and Belgians said that the Community would not be the same again, and the Italians said they were deeply disappointed.

Mr Edward Heath, the leader of the British delegation, put his view plainly:

> We entered these negotiations 16 months ago in good faith and have endeavoured strenuously to reach a successful conclusion. Five countries and the Commission have said publicly that all the remaining problems in the negotiations were capable of solution. I share that view.
>
> The five governments and ourselves all wished to continue the negotiations and bring them to a successful conclusion. The high hopes of so many have thus been thwarted for political reasons at the will of one man. The end of the negotiations is a blow to the cause of that wider European unity for which we have been striving.

Among the Germans, Professor Erhard, the Minister for Economic Affairs, was notably moved. From his performance at his press conference here, there can be no doubt of his strong personal feelings. Professor Erhard said he thought the spirit of the Common Market had been broken. In future its life would be much more mechanical 'The day will dawn,' he said, 'when all six countries will realise we have made a mistake today.' . . .

Before any final news had reached London from Brussels yesterday Mr Macmillan referred, for the first time, to the consequences of a breakdown in the negotiations for Britain's entry into the European Economic Community when he answered questions in the House of Commons.

> If and when they come to an end [he said] a situation will be there which we shall deal with. I am convinced that we shall deal with it as we have always done when we have had difficulties to face. We shall face them, I believe, with a united country.

This 'backs to the wall' mood shows the extent of the upheaval which the Brussels failure will cause in Government policy. Since July 1961, when Mr Macmillan told the House that Britain would apply for negotiations for entry into the Community under the terms of the Treaty of Rome, Government policy—economic, foreign and defence—has been directed on the assumption that Britain would enter the Community. Mr Macmillan had to persuade the Commonwealth Prime Ministers and his own party that this was a proper course for the Government to follow. Now the Government faces the vast disturbance of a readjustment of policies and Mr Macmillan, after his many meetings with President de Gaulle, must take the full responsibility of his complete identification with the policy of Britain's entry.

The Guardian, 30 January, 1963.

De Gaulle and Greater Europe

The curtain has fallen in Brussels—seemingly the final curtain on a European tragedy, though perhaps only the end of an important act. The shock caused by the breach in Brussels will affect the Six themselves as much as the British, and the whole future of Europe's relations with the United States is now in jeopardy. When the repercussions are seen a fresh attempt may be made to bring Britain into Europe. But it cannot happen so long as de Gaulle rules France; nor can the British Government reckon on it as a likelihood. British policy, while trying to keep open the way towards new negotiations with Western Europe must now take a new course.

'This was a European funeral,' the German Vice-Chancellor, Dr Erhard, said after yesterday's meeting. That five of the Six passionately wanted Britain to join is obvious—to all, at any rate, except the President himself. By forcing an abrupt end to the negotiations, by demonstrating that France intends to dominate the Six, by showing that he will not be sorry when the Americans withdraw from Europe, by insisting that Europe must be armed with nuclear weapons in her own right, and by hinting that he will do a deal with Russia President de Gaulle has shattered the concept of a Greater Europe that inspired many of his partners. The effect may have been far stronger than he intended. But the effect is there. The 'European funeral' is not simply the burying of British hopes in Europe. It is also the interment, at least temporarily, of the united Europe that M. Schuman and M. Monnet foresaw.

The Guardian, 30 January 1963.

Bibliography

MANUSCRIPT SOURCES

1 Balfour Papers, British Museum.
2 Lord George Hamilton Papers, India Office Library.
3 Chamberlain Papers, Birmingham University.
4 Earl St Aldwyn (Hicks-Beach) Papers, Williamstrip Park, Gloucestershire.
5 Conference Minutes, Campaign Literature and National Union Gleanings, Conservative Central Office.
6 Collected Speeches and Election Manifestos, National Liberal Club.
 Unless otherwise stated, quotations from speeches are from *The Times*.

BOOKS

7 Abel, Deryk, *History of British Tariffs 1923–42*, Heath Cranton, 1945.
8 Alexander, Eric, *Chief Whip. The Political Life and Times of Aretas Akers-Douglas*, Routledge & Kegan Paul, 1961.
9 Amery, L. S., *My Political Life*, Hutchinson, 1953, vols i and ii.
10 Armitage Smith, G., *The Free Trade Movement and Its Results*, Blackie, 1898.
11 Ashworth, William, *A Short History of The International Economy 1850–1950*, Longmans, 1952.
12 Baldwin, A. W., *My Father: the true story*, Allen & Unwin, 1955.
13 Balfour, Lady Frances, *A Memoir of Lord Balfour of Burleigh*, Hodder & Stoughton, 1924.
14 Blake, Robert, *Life and Times of Andrew Bonar Law*, Eyre & Spottiswoode, 1955.
15 Blake, Robert, *Disraeli*, Eyre & Spottiswoode, 1966.
16 Blewett, N., 'Factionalism within the Unionist Party', *Historical Journal* xi, 1 (1968).

17   Boyd, C. W., *Mr Chamberlain's Speeches*, Constable, 1914.
18   Brooks, Colin, *The Tariff Question*, Arnold, 1931.
19   Brown, B. R., *The Tariff Reform Movement in Great Britain (1881–95)*, New York, 1943.
20   Brown, Lucy, *The Board of Trade and the Free Trade Movement, 1830–42*, Oxford University Press, 1958.
21   Butler, David, and Freeman, Jennie, *British Political Facts 1900–60*, Macmillan, 1964.
22   Cramb, J. A., *Origins and Destiny of Imperial Britain*, Murray, 1915.
23   Cross, Colin, *Philip Snowden*, Barrie & Rockliff, 1966.
24   Davidson, J., *Commercial Federation and Colonial Trade Policy*, Canada, 1900.
25   Dugdale, Blanche, *Arthur James Balfour*, Hutchinson, 1936.
26   Eyre, John Raymond, *The Baldwin Age*, Eyre & Spottiswoode, 1960.
27   Fawcett, Henry, *Free Trade and Protection*, London, 1878.
28   Fraser, Peter, *Joseph Chamberlain*, Cassell, 1966
29   Fraser, Peter, 'The Unionist debacle of 1911 and Mr Balfour's retirement', *Journal of Modern History*, Dec. 1963.
30   Garvin, J. L., and Amery, J., *Life of Joseph Chamberlain*, Macmillan, 1934, 1969, vols. iii to vi.
31   Gash, N. *Politics in the Age of Peel*, Longmans, 1953.
32   Gladwyn, Lord, *The European Idea*, Wiedenfeld & Nicolson, 1966.
33   Gollin, Alfred, *Balfour's Burden*, Blond, 1965.
34   Hewins, W. A. A. *Apologia of an Imperialist*, Constable, 1929, vol. i.
35   Hicks-Beach, Lady Victoria, *Life of Sir Michael Hicks-Beach*, Macmillan, 1932.
36   *Britain and the EEC*, HMSO, 1967.
37   Holland, Bernard, *Life of the Eighth Duke of Devonshire*, Longmans, 1911, vol. 11.
38   Jay, Douglas, *After the Common Market*, Penguin, 1968.
39   Jenkins, Roy, *Mr Balfour's Poodle*, Collins, 1954.
40   Jennings, Sir Ivor, *Party Politics*, vol. i: *Appeal to the People*; vol. iii: *The Stuff of Politics*, Cambridge University Press, 1960.
41   Jeyes, S. H. and How, F. D., *The Life of Sir Howard Vincent*, London, 1912.
42   Judd, Denis, *Balfour and the British Empire*, Macmillan, 1968.

43 Kennedy, A. L., *Salisbury*, Murray, 1953.

44 Kitson Clark, G. *Peel and the Conservative Party*, Bell, 1929.

45 Kitzinger, Uwe, *The European Common Market and Community*, Routledge & Kegan Paul, 1968.

46 Lewis, W. Arthur, *Economic Survey 1919–36*, Allen & Unwin, 1949.

47 Londonderry, Marchioness of, *Henry Chaplin*, Macmillan, 1926.

48 McCready, H. W. 'Revolt of the Unionist Free Traders', *Parliamentary Affairs*, Spring 1963.

49 McCord, Norman, *The Anti-Corn Law League*, Allen & Unwin, 1958.

50 Middlemas, Keith, and Barnes, John, *Baldwin*, Weidenfeld & Nicolson, 1969.

51 Mortimer-Franklin, H., *The Unit of Imperial Federation*, London, 1887.

52 Nicolson, Sir Harold, *George V*, Constable, 1952.

53 Page, W., *Commerce and Industry*, vol. *ii*: *Tables of Statistics for the British Empire from 1815*, Constable, 1919.

54 Packenham, E., *The Jameson Raid*, Weidenfeld & Nicolson, 1960.

55 Petrie, Sir Charles, *Walter Long and his Times*, Hutchinson, 1936.

56 Petrie, Sir Charles, *The Life and Letters of Sir Austen Chamberlain*, Cassell, 1939, vols. i. and ii.

57 Raymond, E. T., *Mr Balfour*, Collins, 1920.

58 Read, Donald, *Cobden and Bright*, Edward Arnold, 1967.

59 Bayers, H. S., *A History of Economic Change in England 1880–1939*, Oxford University Press, 1967.

60 Seeley, J. E., *The Expansion of England*, London, 1918.

61 Skidelsky, Robert, *Politicians and the Slump*, Macmillan, 1967.

62 Smith, Adam, *Wealth of Nations*, Dent, 1967 edition.

63 Spender, J. A., *The Life of Sir Henry Campbell Bannerman*, Hodder & Stoughton, 1923, vol. ii.

64 Uri, Pierre, *From Commonwealth to Common Market*, Penguin, 1968.

65 Williams E. E., *Made in Germany*, Heinemann, 1896.

66 Young, G. M., *Stanley Baldwin*, Hart-Davis, 1952.

67 Young, Kenneth, *Balfour*, Bell, 1963.

Index

145